W9-DBZ-717

Save Them All

Carrie Simon

innovo
PUBLISHING

Published by
Innovo Publishing, LLC
www.innovopublishing.com
1-888-546-2111

Providing Full-Service Publishing Services for
Christian Authors, Artists & Organizations: Hardbacks, Paperbacks,
eBooks, Audiobooks, Music & Film

SAVE THEM ALL

Library of Congress Control Number: 2014948832
ISBN 13: 978-1-61314-240-0

Cover Design & Interior Layout: Innovo Publishing, LLC

Printed in the United States of America
U.S. Printing History

First Edition: October 2014

Dedication

To God, Who has never let me go;

To my children, whom I hold and cherish dearly;

To my husband, family, true friends, and those who bring me inspiration through extraordinary acts of sincere compassion;

To all the children of this world who have been abused in some form or fashion . . . I hear you.

Table of Contents

Chapter 1

On the Porch

The sun sat lazily in the distant sky as they sat on the wooden front porch. It had seen many a year but had weathered them all, though the signs were beginning to show.

Chipped paint around the edges and worn and buckled wood gave it ambience, making it seem almost saddened in reflection, and yet, it made a happy resting place for Ayla to sit and listen. Every now and then, she would come here—her private oasis from school, family, and friends—and listen to the old woman who resided here retell the most extraordinary stories of an era long ago and mostly forgotten by those who hadn't the privilege of living or knowing it.

Sometimes, they would also play backgammon or checkers and drink sweet tea, and other times they would simply discuss her homework or the town's festivals and things such as that.

But whatever the topic, Ayla had taken quite a liking to the old Southern woman. Now granted, she had made a few new friends with which she could discuss boys, life, and such, but she was drawn to the aged woman and her never-ending wealth of knowledge and dry humor. Not because she thought she was old and had perhaps been neglected by the outside world, but quite the contrary, for the woman still possessed so much life. Why, even her demeanor carried such sweet and yet strong character that Ayla found herself wishing should she ever live so long that it would be a sheer delight to have such a sweet disposition as Mrs. Tilly.

She was thin woman, petite and frail, but her eyes were bright and as she spoke, they turned soft and thoughtful, as if she pondered many, many things. In fact, sometimes she would pause in between sentences as if to take another thought or two into consideration and then upon gazing down at her devoted visitor, would begin again with the topic of the day. Her long, gray hair shined like silver strands in the scorching sun, and she constantly brushed them away from her face as she rocked back and forth on a swing that had also seen better days. She had been a widow for some time, yet her late husband's attire had never been removed from the closet nor had his tools ever left the rusty and dilapidated shed that loomed just past the old wooden house in which they had lived for so long. Ayla believed that perhaps they brought comfort to Mrs. Tilly, since she only spoke with kind and loving memories of her late husband. *They must have had a fairy-tale love story*, Ayla thought. *Too bad that doesn't happen these days*, she shrugged. But Ayla never spoke of things like that to Mrs. Tilly, instead choosing mainly to just listen to the stories of old times past.

Ayla paused between sips of the delicious sweet tea and looked at Mrs. Tilly. For some reason, it seemed to her that Mrs. Tilly was not her normal self, almost appearing troubled about something and not conversing as usual. As she continued to watch Mrs. Tilly, she noticed that her hands would tremble in her lap, and she would tilt her head ever so slightly side to side, gaze downward again, then shrug her shoulders and repeat the same behavior.

Before Ayla could question her, the odd gestures came to a halt and Mrs. Tilly spoke. "Well, child, seems as if you grown like a sprout, since the last time I saw you."

Ayla laughed and replied, "Oh, I don't know about that, Mrs. Tilly. I look at myself every day, and I don't see that much of a change," her voice soft and jovial. It had been about a month or so since she had last visited but hardly enough time to speak of change.

She fidgeted with the glass of tea as she spoke, noting that the heat had almost completely dissolved the last of her ice cubes. The wind, however, was finally picking up enough to give some relief from the scorching sun. It had begun to blow her light brown hair around her eyes and slap it softly against her delicate cheeks. She brushed the hairs away without thinking, a burden that was all too common with her long hair. Sometimes it would sting her light green eyes making them water, and Ayla would curse at her hair, but not today. It was only a slight breeze, she mused, and not one to be troubled about.

Mrs. Tilly spoke again, but this time quieter than before. "It's just that today you look so much like her. I mean you could have been her sister if I hadn't known better," her voice choking as she spoke.

"Look like who, Mrs. Tilly?" Ayla asked, unsure if Mrs. Tilly had heard her.

"Her. Well, who else? She was so pretty and so sweet. Lord knows, honey, this little girl was smart too and well behaved. I mean she could have grown up to be anything, why . . . maybe even Miss America!" Mrs. Tilly exclaimed. "Don't tell me you have never heard of her? How long did you say it's been since you and your family moved here?"

Ayla looked directly at Mrs. Tilly, not really sure what to think of the old woman's odd comments. "We moved here almost three years ago, Mrs. Tilly. Are you telling me I have a twin somewhere around here? You got to be kidding me. Why haven't I met her yet? Does she visit with you? Where is she now?" Ayla was suddenly alive with a flurry of questions.

Mrs. Tilly hung her head a little further down but spoke as she did. "You *did* have one, Ayla, at least before you and your family came here. And yes, she used to visit me rather frequently just before you and your family moved here, but she doesn't anymore. Why, it's been years now since all of that. Haven't ever spoken of it since then . . ." Mrs. Tilly said, her voice trailing off as if it were traveling away.

"What," Ayla chimed in, "haven't spoken of what since then, her not visiting you?"

"No," Mrs. Tilly said solemnly as she fixed her gaze upon Ayla. "Her death, my dear . . . her death."

Ayla suddenly felt a chill course through her body, despite the fact that she could still feel the perspiration dripping down the back of her cotton dress. She instantly felt cold and uneasy. Whatever was Mrs. Tilly talking about? The wind began to pick up again, but Ayla didn't notice. She felt slightly more uncomfortable though not really sure and figured if Mrs. Tilly wasn't really going to elaborate any further, not that she necessarily wanted her to, it was the perfect time to leave since she needed to head home anyway.

"Mrs. Tilly," Ayla finally managed to let out, "I think it's about time I head home now. I'll see ya after school tomorrow, if my parents let me."

Mrs. Tilly simply nodded as she lifted herself rather hurriedly from the porch swing and took the glass from Ayla's extended hand. "All right, dear," she said. "Till tomorrow," and with that she disappeared into the wood-frame house past the porch's rickety screen door and down the thin hallway. Ayla, looking one last time at Mrs. Tilly's fleeting frame, picked up her book sack and walked the rest of the dusty, gravel road for about half a mile until she arrived home.

Once inside her home, the mood was different. Ayla had many siblings, and since her mother had decided to return to college late in life, Ayla now had the responsibility of their care. Setting her book sack to the side, she began to tidy up the house little by little and prepare dinner.

Although she really wasn't hungry, she knew she should go ahead and start cooking for everyone else who may be. Her father would soon be home and would want to have something on the table after working all day.

As she began to pull items from the pantry, she tried to shake the thought of Mrs. Tilly from her head, but she could not. The old woman seemed so sad and forlorn as they spoke today.

Maybe she was close to the girl, Ayla thought. *Maybe I should ask her to explain what happened. Perhaps she never had anyone to talk to other than that girl after her husband's death.* More thoughts continued to swirl about in her head. But the more she thought about it, the more uneasy she became. Ayla continued to try to shrug it off and put the large slab of meat into the pan, letting it sizzle and brown in the sugar and oil. Next, she put the rice into the cooker and took a couple of canned vegetables from the rear pantry in the kitchen to add to the meal. Putting them separately into pots, she then began to straighten the dining room where they would soon be sitting and eating. She could hear her siblings talking amongst themselves in the background. *They must all be in the family room,*

Ayla thought, and went back to the stove to stir the vegetables and look over the meat and rice.

"Hey," Ayla called out, "make sure y'all finish your homework and clean up before dinner. Dad should be back in a half hour."

Ayla's sister was the first to respond, jumping into the kitchen with a happy gait. "Of course, *Mom*," she said sarcastically, but playfully.

"Come on, Sis," Ayla retorted with a snort, "cut me some slack. You know I hate sounding bossy, but that's better than Dad's fussing and besides . . . I'm doing the best I can."

"I know, Sis. Just thought I'd tease you for a bit. Don't get so uptight about all of this. Mom will soon take over again and you can go back to thinking about boys and looking in the mirror," she giggled. Ayla smiled as she looked at her sister. She was right; it was only for another few months or so, then everything would be okay and once again allow her to just be a normal teenager.

"Okay," Ayla replied. "You are right. Now go tell your brothers to do what they're supposed to, and then come have dinner when it's ready."

Ayla's sister hurried out of the room quite happy to be given the job of ordering the other siblings about. Ayla finished with the tidying of the kitchen and moved into the other rooms, one by one straightening them a little more for her father's inspection and approval. Once she had finished, she went back into the kitchen to finish cooking dinner. She knew she still had her own homework to do, but that would have just to wait. She had an important test in her history class, and she would need some serious alone time to study and be prepared.

Ayla's father was kind but strict, and he was very adamant that everyone do well in school. Academics first, sports second, was his motto. The idea of anything other than an A wasn't ever an option. So Ayla knew she had to get in at least one hour of uninterrupted study time if she was going to do well on Mr. Curtis' test tomorrow.

Once she had stirred everything again on the stove and was satisfied that everything was ready to be served, she heard her father's old van coming down the long, sloping driveway. *Just in time*, she thought with a sigh of relief. Now, everyone could eat together, and if she cleaned up quickly and made sure they all took their baths, she would have enough time to study before bed.

Her father's briefcase struck the door as Ayla heard him turning the knob. "Ayla," he called out, "think you could help me?" Ayla ran to the door and pulled it just as her father was pushing. He had grocery bags in one hand, his briefcase in the other. Ayla grabbed the grocery bags from his hands and ushered him in.

"Here, Dad!" Ayla exclaimed, "I made some dinner. It's ready, if you're hungry."

Ayla's dad, James, let out a loud sigh as he smiled and walked past her and down the stairs to a room he had made into his office. Ayla could tell it had been a long day by the look in his eyes. He was tired and exhausted once again, and Ayla wondered just how long he could continue heading out early in the mornings to court, attending numerous hearings, only to come home and type his own pleadings. *He could use a secretary*, she thought, even if he didn't want to admit it. Sometimes, Ayla would awaken in the wee hours of the morning to the sounds of his old typewriter and be comforted by its sound because it had been so familiar to her growing up. Ayla's thoughts began to drift for a moment, but then she reminded herself of the dinner and, pursing her lips together, opened up the cabinet and took out a stack of plates from the top shelf. Setting them on the corner of the table she began to allot one to each of the seats at the table. She finished setting them all out on the table and pulled the silverware from the drawer. She set them all nicely by each plate and then the napkins. She also set a glass by each plate to finish. "Finally," she said quietly to herself, scanning the dining room with a look of approval and satisfaction. Now, everyone could eat. Ayla never ate too much when she had things on her mind. Sometimes she'd have to remind herself to eat because the hunger was an afterthought when other things were more important to her, like the test she had to study for or the strange uneasiness that Mrs. Tilly's comments made.

It was one that only aroused her curiosity and yet something was sinister about it, or Ayla would not have found it so unnerving. Just the way Mrs. Tilly had looked at her at when she had seen her earlier today had made her feel odd. Almost like she had been looking right through her, not really seeing her, somewhere locked in those deep thoughts of hers that Ayla was still too nervous to ask her about.

Ayla's brothers were the first to come up the stairs, and like typical boys, they began grabbing the plates off the table in an urgent fashion and were soon standing in line near the stove where they would put heaping and hot spoonfuls of the food on their plates. Ayla sat back, letting them finish, the smell of the homemade Southern food lingering in the air and bringing a warmth and unity from it that always made her smile.

Ayla's sister patted her back as she walked through the kitchen and headed to the table to pick up her plate as the boys sat down with theirs. "Wow!" she said looking around. "I'm surprised there's even any left after all that." She pointed a small finger at their plates, pretending to look disgusted.

Ayla laughed aloud. "There should be enough, Sis. Though, not everyone has eaten yet and we have to leave some for Mom." Ayla's sister walked to the stove still mumbling to herself as she dished smaller portions onto her plate and brought it to the table. Ayla watched them as they all patiently waited in their chairs, the steam rising from their plates, yet not a spoon or fork moved from its place as if held by a force unspoken. Ayla knew why; they were all waiting on their father.

Some of her siblings began to fidget in their seats but quickly stopped when they saw their father's face peering at them directly.

"Waiting on me?" he said tiredly. Everyone nodded and Ayla handed him his plate. He accepted it from her hands and headed toward the kitchen to gather what was left of the prepared food. He reappeared only moments later with his plate in hand loaded with the delicious smelling food. As he sat down, he let out another long sigh. He looked around the room and positioned his hands together on the table. "Shall we pray?" he said, suddenly serious, and the room became silent out of respect.

They all bowed their heads in prayer, and Ayla's father began. "Lord, we come to You this evening and we thank You for all that You have provided. Please bless this food that we are about to consume, and lead us and guide us in Your ways. Be with us and protect us. In Your name, we ask all these things. Amen."

Ayla's father looked up again and around the room. As he did, he smiled again tiredly, yawning at the same time. Ayla thought that just for a moment he wasn't thinking about work, life, and stress. Maybe he was just thinking about all of them. It was a lofty idea even if it wasn't realistic.

Ayla's father, brothers, and sister began to eat. For a few minutes, the clicking of their silverware was the only sound. Then as in unison, they began speaking of the day, what they had done, their homework, school events, etc. No one noticed that Ayla still had no plate in front of her. In fact, Ayla was able to simply drift slowly away from the livelihood of the dining room and toward the kitchen, satisfied to simply bask in the warmth of conversation that dinner provided, if not her appetite.

She pulled a large, white dinner plate down from the shelf and fixed the remaining food for her mother, setting it in the microwave for her to warm up when she returned from a long night of studying. There hadn't been much left in the pots, so Ayla was glad that no one had questioned the fact that she had not eaten, this way her mother would have something to eat. Ayla began gathering the pots and rinsing them all in the sink. She filled up the sink with water and squirted some detergent into the basin. As she scrubbed them with her hands, the hot water felt good against her delicate skin. Ayla hummed to herself as she washed the pots, set a cloth on the counter, and put them there on the cloth to dry.

It wasn't long before her brothers had each brought his dirty plate into the kitchen and put them into the dishwater with a smile.

"Sure was good, Sis," her brother John called out as he backed away from the sink.

Ayla laughed aloud, "Glad you enjoyed it. Next time, you can do the cooking."

He laughed back, "Yeah, right, you know I can't cook . . . but I sure can eat," and he rubbed his little belly with appreciation.

"I know," Ayla said. "Just thought I'd tease you with the idea."

The rest put their plates into the sudsy water and gave their compliments. Ayla felt tired, but happy. She liked tending to everyone. Perhaps she was a nurturer like her mother used to call her. She did have a knack for things like this, but the idea of having her own children one day was the last thing on her mind. She was too busy with sports, schoolwork, and hanging out with her friends. Every once in a while, her friends would tease her for visiting Mrs. Tilly, but she didn't mind. She would tell them that she liked helping her do things, but really she went to spend time with her. She liked her and was happy to have a companion who was not as judgmental as her friends or her parents sometimes.

Once the other dishes were finished, Ayla began drying them and putting them away. She wiped down the countertops and the dining room table. Turning off the lights, she walked toward her bedroom. The room was dark and cold. Ayla turned on the light switch and threw her book sack onto the bed. It hit with a thud and bounced for a moment before resting like a heavy boulder. Ayla pulled her shoes off and jumped quickly on the bed, sitting with her legs crossed as she unzipped the book sack and pulled the books out of it. Her notebook also sat beside her along with her pencils and her journal that was off limits to everyone but her. In fact, it was more than a journal. Ayla likened it to a "thought collector."

Whether she was in school or not, if she thought of something worth remembering, she would pull it out and jot down her thoughts. But there was no time for that now; she could write down her thoughts about what Mrs. Tilly had said later when she had more time.

The history book lay the farthest from her, so she stretched out and lunged across the bed, grasping it with her hand and turning to the appropriate pages. The lesson had been about world presidents and their rise to political status. Ayla had taken good notes, but she really wasn't interested in studying. She pulled the notebook up toward her and went directly to the notes.

Four pages had been dedicated to the lecture, and Ayla began perusing each of her answers to the questions. The teacher hadn't said which ones would be on the test, so Ayla knew he probably planned to ask all of them. *Hope it's multiple choice*, Ayla thought. She sat on her bed for over an hour, memorizing the pages in her head before glancing at the clock. It was past 9:30 p.m., and she hadn't even gone to take her bath. She finished up the rest of her homework and put it all, along with the books, back into the book sack. Then she grabbed some pajamas and panties from the chest of drawers and walked quietly into the bathroom.

She closed the door behind her and sat the clothes on the counter by the sink. She turned on the warm water in the tub and began taking off her shirt and jeans. They had begun to hang loosely around her already small frame, but no one yet had noticed. Ayla thought it made her prettier when she saw her ribs protruding from her sides. *Now, I look like a model,* Ayla thought studying herself again and again in the mirror, wondering what Mrs. Tilly had seen in her today. The mirror only revealed her straight brown hair as it hung loosely about her shoulders, her green eyes staring widely back at her, and her pale skin looking like porcelain. Nothing out of the ordinary, right?

Why the look in Mrs. Tilly's eyes? Had she really changed all that much since her last visit? There were those who found her pretty. In fact, all her friends said so, but Ayla did not feel it. She always pinched and poked at herself, sucking her stomach in and out trying to embody an idealistic beauty that she might just perhaps attain. But she was already petite and slim, perhaps a bit too lean for her age, but in her adolescent eyes, only the imperfections mattered. She noticed that the bathtub had begun to fill up with warm water, so she turned the faucets off and put one foot in after the other, slowly sitting down in the swirling water, and laid her head back against the tub. Boy, the water felt good. It had been a long day and tomorrow would be no different. Same chores, same responsibilities, same faces surrounding her throughout the day. Ayla now knew what was expected of her until her mother finished school. But who could blame her for enjoying a quiet moment all to herself? Ayla closed her eyes trying to drift away from all of that. Her mother would soon be home and Ayla wanted to be in bed before that. She finished shaving her legs and washing her hair and body with the heavily scented soap her aunt had given her. Then she stood up and let the remaining warm water gingerly drain out of the tub.

She grabbed the large towel from the adjacent rack and slipped it around her body as she stepped out of the tub. With her floral pajamas on and her hair brushed, she quickly straightened the bathroom and scampered to her room. Once there, she slid underneath the covers and drifted to sleep, with her mind still racing.

Chapter 2

Back on the Porch

The first rays of sunlight streamed in through the window facing Ayla's bed. At first, she pretended not to notice them, but eventually she had no choice but to face the fact that she needed to get out of bed and begin getting ready for school. She moaned and groaned as she stretched her arms out in a feline manner contemplating what to wear, but then sat up and began to go through the motions of pulling down the covers and stepping out onto the rug that nestled beside her bed. At first, she had been reluctant to get out of bed, but now that she was, she had awakened enough to realize she had slept a little longer than usual and would have to hurry a bit if she wanted to catch the bus with her brothers and sister.

She walked hurriedly to the bathroom to brush her teeth and hair. Once finished, she looked rather forlornly into the mirror, once again dissatisfied with the face looking back, and turned off the light with disgust. She then pulled a pair of her favorite jeans and a t-shirt from the closet. Though baggy, these jeans always made her feel relaxed. Slipping a pair of tennis shoes on after quickly making her bed, she gave herself a quick glance in the mirror and ran hurriedly down the stairs to join her siblings.

The kitchen was already alive with chatter as Ayla's brothers began to pour cereal into their bowls. Ayla opened the fridge, ignoring the clicking and clattering, and retrieved a container of juice. She had made the juice the other day from some fresh fruits out of the garden and wasn't really all that hungry. Ayla's mom put her arm on Ayla as she began to pour the contents of the container into a small oval-shaped glass.

"Ayla," her mother began, "not hungry again this morning? I sure wish you would eat something. I mean you look smaller since just yesterday." Ayla looked at her mom and then back down at the glass as she mumbled to herself. She hated these conversations. If only her mother would just leave her alone about it, maybe it would be easier. *Why can't she see I just want to be pretty?* Ayla thought. She looked back up again at her mother. She knew deep down that her mother loved her; it just seemed lately everything she did was wrong. What was so bad about being skinny anyway? Ayla couldn't stand the idea of being fat.

"Look, Mom," Ayla stammered. "I'm fine, really. I just don't have that much of an appetite. I gotta big test today, we're preparing for our next volleyball game, and I promised Mrs. Tilly I would come over after school and help her out around the house and stuff."

Ayla's mother backed away and paused for a moment. "Well then, young lady, I guess you had better eat something so you don't get exhausted from all of that!" Ayla knew her mother was not going to budge, so she picked up a bowl and, filling it halfway with cereal, munched the breakfast in silence.

Soon the rumbling sound of the bus could be heard in the distance. "Better head up there," Ayla's mother said, looking at Ayla. Ayla could feel her eyes boring into her, but she did not know why. The bus ride left much to be desired as she sat in silence, but once she had arrived at school, the atmosphere was almost frenzied.

Various school officials passed to and fro in the massive halls as herds of students all scurried to their appropriate classes, darting past her. The school was a pleasant one. Most of her teachers were nice and helpful, and Ayla was pretty popular for only having lived in the area for so short a period. She remembered being hesitant when she had first set eyes on the school, knowing she was an outsider and perhaps a bit nervous about being one. But they had all somewhat warmed up soon enough, though some kids still eyed her oddly. Ayla's dad and mom had gone out of their way to invite many of the children and their parents over to visit. Although it had been a strain on their already taxing careers, Ayla was pleased they had gone to such lengths to make her and her siblings comfortable with the move. After a few months, Ayla had begun to open up to all her new friends and tried out for the volleyball team and cheerleading squad. Much to her amazement, she had been selected for both. She remembered coming home and telling her mother. Ayla closed her eyes for a moment and drifted back to that day. She recalled her mother's voice of surprise and the pride she felt when her mother had put her arms around her, congratulating her. How happy she had felt that day, like she belonged at the school, like she felt connected to this town.

"Ayla, are you with us today?" Ayla looked up and peered over her hand, which she had propped against her head while in thought. It was Ayla's homeroom teacher, Mrs. Allen, who had spoken. Ayla's face blushed red at the acknowledgment of the voice. She could see by this point that all the eyes in the room were looking at her.

"Yes, Mrs. Allen, I'm here. I'm sorry. I really didn't hear you call my name," Ayla spoke softly.

"Well, next time try to get some sleep the night before, and maybe you will be alert enough to hear your name being called," Mrs. Allen snapped.

Ayla nodded to avoid further embarrassment, slid her body further down in her desk, and picked up one of her schoolbooks to read. After a few minutes, she scanned the room and realized the students had stopped glancing in her direction and continued to carry on with their studies. Ayla felt relieved. She had felt their eyes on her as Mrs. Allen ridiculed her for daydreaming. *Bet they don't have siblings to care for like I do and a house to run*, Ayla thought. "Oh well, never mind about them; who cares?" she mumbled to herself and focused again on the school lesson.

After some brief discussions on grammar and literature, Mrs. Allen put down the chalk from the chalkboard and ordered her homework for the night. As soon as she had uttered the final word of instructions, the bell rang loudly through each and every classroom, so that a new class in a separate subject could begin. Out in the hall, Ayla began to play out the rest of her day in her head. Next class was biology, then math, and after that the history test that she had stayed up late for in order to make the grade that she had promised her father. The day was starting to pick up and before too long, she would be home to visit with Mrs. Tilly.

Ayla's last class was history with Mr. Curtis. He was a quiet man with small spectacles that inched way down his nose so his eyes could glare intently through them, though he did not do that too often. For the most part, Ayla concurred that he was a very smart and kind teacher.

Everyone had shuffled into the classroom and sat down in his or her respective chairs. Ayla sat down as well and pulled her book sack shut, only grabbing her No. 2 pencil and setting it in the small indentation on the top of the desk. Since today was the test only, there was really no sense in pulling anything else out of the book sack. She looked around the room at all the other students her age. There was a wide variety of varying faces. Ayla studied them quickly, squinching her eyes and nose as she did.

Mr. Curtis entered the classroom. "Good afternoon, class," he began. "As you know, we will be having a test today, so if you have anything other than a pencil on your desk, I strongly suggest you put it away, as I will be handing out the test in a minute and will fail anyone who still has anything on the desk other than his or her pencil." Mr. Curtis could be strict sometimes. Everyone began scrambling, though it did not take long to finish. Soon he was passing the pages of the test back and forth on the rows of seats that were centered in the room. Each student began putting pages together and looked hesitantly at the writing on them. Once he had finished, Mr. Curtis went to his chair behind the desk and sat down. "You may begin," he said to the class, and Ayla paused only for a moment because she had already started.

The long hour finished with everyone turning in his or her tests upon leaving the classroom. Only a few hmms and umms interrupted the concentration of many of the others, but instead of turning it in and getting out early, Ayla had stayed and reviewed every answer and question thoroughly. There were a few that perhaps were not correct, but they had seemed the most logical, so she had not amended her original answers. As it neared the end of the hour, Ayla approached Mr. Curtis and handed him the papers.

He looked up and smiled, "How do you think you did, Ms. Ayla?"

"I'm not sure," Ayla said, "but I think I did okay," Ayla muttered, smiling back.

Mr. Curtis laughed aloud. "I'm sure you did. I looked up early and realized you had finished writing but did not get up to leave. Thought I'd ask."

It was Ayla's turn to laugh a little as she spoke. "Yep, I was, but I wanted to make sure I hadn't answered in a hurry without thinking." She lifted her book sack and followed the other students out of his class and to her own homeroom to wait for school dismissal.

Ayla finally caught up with her brothers and sister as she headed for the bus to take them home, taking a quick seat near her sister. "Hey, Sis," Ayla called out. "I promised Mrs. Tilly I would come back and speak to her today after school. Tell Dad, okay?"

Ayla's sister nodded. "Sure, but why are you going back so soon? Does she need that much help? She looks pretty active to me." Ayla commented to herself how wise and observant her little sister was. It was true; Mrs. Tilly could take care of herself. *Maybe*, she thought, *I should invite my sis to come see Mrs. Tilly and hear her stories. Just not now.* Right now, that was Ayla's private comfort.

"She can, I just help her out a bit," Ayla heard herself say.

"All right, Ayla, I'll tell Dad. Just don't stay too long. I'm already hungry for dinner," she giggled. Ayla smiled and giggled back, promising that she would return with a few hours.

The bus began dropping the children one by one at their respective homes. Mrs. Tilly's house was not far from theirs, so Ayla could walk quickly home after the visit. She was caught up in her thoughts of hearing what Mrs. Tilly had wanted to tell her that she almost forgot to step up and tell the bus driver where she needed to be dropped off. Mr. Don Terrence was a grumpy bus driver who did not even seem to like hearing the children's constant chatter and commotion. So Ayla was a bit nervous as she tried to approach the front of the bus.

"Mr. Don," Ayla called out, holding on to the back of the seat in order to keep from falling as the bus rode down the bumpy country road. "I need to get off at Mrs. Tilly's house. It's the last one on the left down this road."

Mr. Don looked over his shoulder and grimaced. "All right, same house as last time?"

"Yes, sir!" Ayla exclaimed. Ayla gave each of her siblings a quick hug and a wave goodbye as the bus left a cloud of dust and disappeared further down the road.

Mrs. Tilly was not on the front porch as usual, so Ayla walked up the steps and tapped the screen door. "Mrs. Tilly," Ayla called out. "Mrs. Tilly, it's Ayla, I'm here." Mrs. Tilly arrived a few moments later at the door with a pitcher of her delicious tea and a couple of glasses. Ayla pulled open the screen door, grabbed the pitcher from her hands, and set it down on one of the little end tables that decorated her wooden porch. Mrs. Tilly sat down on the swing and pulled a handkerchief from out of one of her pockets in her floral housedress. She began wiping the sweat that had beaded up on her forehead and muttered to herself something inaudible to Ayla.

"Well, dearie, glad you returned. For a moment, I thought I'd have no one to drink my tea with," she said.

"Oh, Mrs. Tilly, I would never just not come. Besides, I promised you I would. It was just a little longer than usual on the bus today. Why, we didn't even make it to Plum Street until after 3:00." Mrs. Tilly smiled and then paused again, obviously going to and from light conversation to deep thoughts. Usually Ayla would just wait and sip her tea when Mrs. Tilly would do this. It did no good to interrupt her behavior. She was almost incoherent when she would be lost in thought. So, Ayla just stopped talking for a moment and looked around. Mrs. Tilly had one of the most eclectic yards in the neighborhood. Little figurines and pinwheels lined the yard in an almost whimsical fashion. They all must have had a special meaning, but to most, they would have seemed tacky and deplorable.

However, Mrs. Tilly wasn't too worried about other people's ideas. To her, they were perfect and she never seemed too tired of going to the local flea market and fetching another one for her small yard.

Ayla looked back at Mrs. Tilly. She took a sip of her tea and glanced down, still trying to be patient with Mrs. Tilly.

"Oh, Ayla, I'm sorry," Mrs. Tilly said finally with a sigh. "That happens more than I'd like to admit these days."

Ayla smiled apologetically at Mrs. Tilly. "It's okay; I do that sometimes and I'm only fifteen."

Mrs. Tilly laughed a little at that and put her glass down on the table. "Ayla," she said, "remember what I was talking about yesterday? Well, I think we should just leave that alone for now. No sense in thinking of such sad things on another beautiful sunny day."

Ayla frowned. Yesterday, Mrs. Tilly had seemed so anxious to tell her something important, and now it was as if she was trying her best to avoid it. "That's fine, Mrs. Tilly," Ayla said, somewhat disappointingly. "No sense in talking about something you don't want to. There are all kinds of things I want to ask you. Like how you met your husband. What was dating like back then? Did you have a job or did you keep yourself busy as a homemaker?" Ayla keep rattling on and Mrs. Tilly interrupted impatiently.

"Ayla, Ayla, pick one; we've only an hour to chat before you have to head home. I can't possibly tell you all of those things in one sittin'!" Mrs. Tilly said rather abruptly.

"Oh, all right," Ayla whispered." I'm sorry, Mrs. Tilly. It's just all your stories are so interesting. It fascinates me the way people used to live. The slowness of it all, the peacefulness."

"Peaceful, eh?" Mrs. Tilly replied with a look. "Honey, it may have been a bit slower, but it was definitely not easy or peaceful. Why, when I met my late husband he had just returned from the Korean War. Many of my friends and I had begun sewing in a large factory not far from here. We would sew all kinds of things and work late, late hours. Sometimes, I would come home and my fingers would be numb. But I didn't complain because I needed the money and was eager for the work. Once I had finished high school, the logical thing had been to get a different job and earn an honest living. So, I applied for a bookkeeping position. I remember always accepting extra shifts when they'd offer. I was eager to earn the money while I could. Me, my friend Doralee, and one other, whose name I can't recall, all stayed in a small flat down on 9th Street so we could be close to the factory. Doralee wasn't much of a worker, but she was company and it beat going to a show alone."

"Show?" Ayla questioned.

"Yes, that's what they used to call the movies back then. Didn't cost as much as it does now, and they still took better care of the place," Mrs. Tilly replied.

"Oh," Ayla said and then hushed so that Mrs. Tilly could continue.

"So," she said as she *hmmphed* and put her hands on her hips, "me and Doralee would catch a show every now and then, but she was always wanting to go places that I didn't care to. I wanted to save my money, not spend it. The other girl and Doralee had to go. Now, granted, they were none too pleased. But it was my little apartment and neither one of them would have been able to keep up the rent, so I kicked them out. For a long time afterward, Doralee refused to speak to me at work. She would purposely ignore me when some of the other ladies and I would eat our lunches in the small break room just down the hall from where we worked. I knew she was upset with me for not letting them stay, but I was tired of them taking advantage of me, and the fact that she was still holding a grudge only further reminded me why I had made that decision. Many months went on, working late hours and being ignored by old friends until one day, or should I say one night, when I was turning off the small light by my desk, a hand on my back liked to have given me a heart attack, so I jumped and turned around. It was my boss, Cecil. A small man with beady eyes who was actually shorter in stature than me. He looked at me and with a glare told me to sit back down. I'll admit, I was scared, really I was. Not really of him but of losing my job, my apartment, and my things. They all flashed in my mind in an instant but disappeared as he put his hands back on my shoulders. 'Hush now,' he said. 'This will be over in a minute.'

"I felt his hands slip from my shoulders down to the buttons of my blouse. I literally felt frozen like a mannequin waiting for him to leave so I could run. He cupped the left side of my breast, and I jumped out of my seat again. 'Sit down, you,' he said gruffly. It sounded more like a snarl than words, but I refused. I pushed him with as much strength as I could muster and grabbed my purse and overcoat. I stormed out of the office and ran as fast as I could down the broken and dilapidated sidewalk toward the apartment. I remember wishing that I could just grow a pair of wings or something. I even thought Mr. Cecil might be right behind me if I turned around, so I ran and ran until I got there. Scrambling in my purse, I retrieved the keys and let myself in. I locked the door behind me and instantly fell to my knees beside it. I did not turn on the lights for a few hours, instead allowing myself to fumble around in the house in the dark, just in case Mr. Cecil had been following me. I knew this was silly, but I was scared. In an instant, everything in my little world had changed. I began to cry and drifted to sleep as I tried to figure out how I was gonna pay rent that month.

"The next morning wasn't much better, since I had only traded my feelings of fear and dread into uneasiness and uncertainty for the future. Should I return? Should I try to move and find a new job? At that time in my life, I was young and there wasn't much available to women. I resolved to face my misgivings and demand that Mr. Cecil be fired. I was pretty sure that I had not been the only girl he had bothered in such a fashion. There had to be someone who was his super, perhaps they would listen to me, and maybe I would still be able to keep my job.

"That afternoon as the hour drew closer for my normal shift, my stomach turned and anxiety grew, but I left anyway. Once there, I did not sit at my desk but marched with defiance toward the main office where there was a small desk and a small fan that did more buzzing than blowing. A small lady sat behind the counter with her ear pressed to a large black phone, and as she spoke into the receiver, she pulled a long strand of pink ooze that she would roll up and down on one of her fingers and then begin chewing in a frenzy. She had hardly looked up until I was there rapping on the side of the entryway to get her attention."

Chapter 3

The Dream

"What happened next, Mrs. Tilly?" Ayla asked, her voice eager with the anticipation of the rest of the story.

"Well," Mrs. Tilly said haughtily, "they accused me of being a liar about that li'l weasel of a man, Mr. Cecil, and fired me on the spot. Seems he had already given them his side of the story before I had gotten there. Perhaps if I had gotten the gumption earlier, things would have been different. But nevertheless, hopefully the fact that I was not afraid to tell the truth may have helped other ladies he had taken advantage of."

Ayla breathed a long sigh. The story was interesting, but it had taken longer than she thought. She had better head home now. She would need to finish her chores and start cooking and, from the looks of it, the sun was already starting to set.

"I wish I could sit here for hours, Mrs. Tilly," Ayla said as she wiped off her pants and stood up. Her glass of tea had been finished quite some time ago, but she hadn't noticed as Mrs. Tilly relived some of her life. She sat it on the small table by Mrs. Tilly's glass and the large pitcher.

"Want me to help you clean this up?" Ayla said, pointing to the dirty dishes.

"Heavens no, dear!" Mrs. Tilly exclaimed. "Of course not, you're a guest." She began mumbling under her breath and hurriedly tried to pick them all up by herself. Ayla could not help but giggle. It was obvious that Mrs. Tilly was having a bit of difficulty. *Stubborn woman*, Ayla thought, *but proud*. Ayla admired that about Mrs. Tilly. She was the kind of woman who wasn't afraid of hard work and doing things on her own.

Ayla reached out and grabbed the glasses as they started to slip through Mrs. Tilly's fingers. "Can't help it, Mrs. Tilly, just wouldn't be right not helping you and everything."

"Well, all right," Mrs. Tilly said indignantly. But the look on her face was a relieved one. Although she didn't say it, Ayla knew in her heart that Mrs. Tilly enjoyed her company as well. Even if she was all right being alone, it wasn't the same as wanting to be. Ayla brought in the glasses and looked about the rooms in Mrs. Tilly's house. Porcelain figures, old antiques, and lots of dusty knickknacks cluttered the rooms. It was like a small store inside with rows and rows of interesting finds, but there was no time to stop and look, so she smiled back at Mrs. Tilly and walked toward the front door.

"Bye, Mrs. Tilly. I'll come again soon," Ayla called out loudly, though not quite sure if she had heard. She needed to get home and fast. It was now starting to get dark and she did not want her father to be angry or worried. Her normal gait wasn't going to cut it tonight, so she put her book sack around her shoulders tightly and began to sprint home.

This night wasn't much different than the evening before, though Ayla did remind herself to eat a few bites at the dinner table since she had noticed another dizzy spell coming on. As the night wore on, she quickly finished her chores and took a nice long bath to relax. *Thank goodness I haven't been given much homework to do*, she thought as she sprawled across her bed and drifted to sleep. Before another hour had passed, her eyes fluttered and she began to dream. Normally, her dreams were happy. Sometimes a little too busy, but always happy. Typically, they would involve a promotion or an accolade of some sort or in some, she would be in some sort of race. They were so common that Ayla found them comforting and would usually go to bed at night with the thought of either a race or an award on her mind.

Tonight, however, was not the same, nor would it ever be again. Unlike her normal dreams of praise and adoration, this one was different. As Ayla dreamt, her thoughts were plagued by the vision of a strange girl. She was tall and lean with a sad countenance, dark brown eyes, and long stringy brown hair that reached to the middle of her back. Ayla did not recognize her but felt as if she needed to follow her. Every time the girl would appear, Ayla would pursue her until she seemed to vanish. Each time that Ayla would catch up to her, she would disappear only to reappear in another setting. Ayla tried calling out to her, but the girl did not speak, only drifted to and from destinations as if she were floating.

At first, she appeared in a field of small, yellow flowers. Ayla could feel the tips of the soft flowers as they swayed in a gentle warm breeze. The girl began copying Ayla's movements and motions while staring back at her. Although Ayla was taken aback by the presence of the strange girl, she was not uncomfortable nor sensed any danger from her. Then just as she was feeling the tenderness of the flowers and the breathtaking view of the meadow, she felt herself running faster as she began chasing the girl again to a small house in the distance. It stood all by itself, and it did not feel very welcoming. Ayla felt a chill as she drew closer to the girl. She was motioning with her hands to come closer. Ayla began walking cautiously toward her and called out to her, but again there was no reply from the strange visitor.

The house was ancient, with broken and torn pieces of wood that held it together. The whole house looked smaller than her and her sister's rooms combined. The door itself squeaked while holding on by a single hinge at the top of its frame. It was rusty and looked like it would fall with the slightest breeze. Ayla followed the girl around the yard surrounding the sinister house. The weeds and grass had grown high and looming. Ayla thought she saw toys between the long blades of grass but could not be sure. Were there children nearby? Ayla saw no darting movements from the home and heard no sounds, only an eerie and strange uneasiness that seemed to radiate from its very frame, as if the house itself embodied an unspoken evilness with no name. Ayla tried yet another time to catch up, but this time she suddenly felt a wave of nausea and paused to rest because she felt sick, queasy, and uncomfortable. At first, she thought she had traveled into a dark tunnel, small and cramped, but then her narrowed eyes refocused to reveal the same type of wood she had seen on the outside of the worn-down house. She instantly knew they were no longer outside but rather on the inside somehow.

Ayla couldn't believe she had followed her inside the creepy house! Ayla's eyes began to flutter even faster and her hands raised up unawares to fend off whatever invisible demons she could, though in her dream she was still trying to reach the girl and put an end to all of this. She put her outstretched arms down and looked around. The little girl had disappeared again and for a moment, Ayla felt alone, scared, almost panicked. A small light began to flicker in what Ayla had thought was a closet. Slowly she forced herself to walk toward the light and there sat the girl. A small, tiny bed or cot lay on the side of the room. It looked more like a mattress with no frame holding it up off the cold, dark floor. There were no covers on it, nor any tables surrounding it. The smell alone was repulsive and reminded Ayla of something decayed. With further scrutiny, Ayla noticed that it and a few bundles of clothes scattered across the little room were the only things in it. Ayla tried to turn away from it, but the little girl sat staring back at her on the decrepit bed and motioned again with her hand to come and sit. Ayla was mesmerized by the surroundings, but her will would not allow her to simply do as she was told. She already felt as if the evil in the house was trying to seep into her skin. She felt as if she was suffocating and she wanted out. She finally managed to walk away from the room and the strange girl, instantly reappearing outside much to her relief. Already she felt out of breath, and she turned her back to the creepy house, refusing to give it another glance.

However, it wasn't long before she could feel another presence. It was the girl again, but this time she looked even more contrite than before. She beckoned Ayla to another place close to a small embankment near a large pond. It looked like a diminutive thicket jutting out with overgrown grass and gnarled branches that had fallen and lay scattered about. By the embankment, she seemed to stop again as if waiting for Ayla to catch up. Ayla again felt a tightening in her chest and a shortness of breath. It was a beautiful scene but overwhelmingly sad. She could sense something different in the eyes of the little girl. Now they stared back at her with more dread and hopelessness. Ayla continued to reach for the girl, but something was happening to her now, and this time she did not instantly vanish. A dark cloud began to swirl about her lean figure. She felt herself frightened for the girl but could not seem to move, as if paralyzed. Even as the cloud continued to widen and engulf the strange figure, Ayla could only call out to her. The girl began to hold her hands out through the swirling air in Ayla's direction, once again trying to motion for her. Ayla could see the girl's eyes distinctly as she tried to lessen the space between them. Sprinting closer, Ayla appeared light as a feather. *Maybe I can reach her now,* she thought. She struggled to move faster in time, but the dream was on its own pace. The cloud was now thickening and Ayla yelled out again to the girl, unable to see her any longer. Although she did not understand it, she could empathize with the pain and fear of the girl, striving to be free of the danger.

"Please . . . I only want to help," Ayla called out. The beautiful stranger was almost gone but not before she reached out one last time to Ayla. It was then that Ayla realized that the strange girl's fingers were completely gone from her hands, and her mouth kept repeating the same words. Too stunned at the revelation, Ayla began to scream wildly.

Ayla's mom was the first to come running. Upon hearing the screams, she had rushed down the stairs without even thinking. As a mother, she knew the sound of each of her children's voice. Instinctively she knew it was her daughter Ayla, and she sounded like she was in pain. What was going on? She pushed open the door and shuddered as a chill ran down her spine; the room was as cold as ice. Ayla lay in her bed above the covers, drenched with sweat and holding on to a soft, dark pillow whimpering like a small defenseless animal. Ayla's mother could hear just above the whimpers, Ayla's voice mumbling something in the dark, barely audible, but definitely words. She reached for Ayla and Ayla put her hands out into the frozen darkness. "Mom," Ayla whispered, "is that you?" Ayla's mother turned on the light switch and immediately light flooded the small bedroom.

"Yes, baby, what's wrong?" Ayla's mother asked as she stroked her daughter's hair. It was damp and cold. As she let her hand fall onto the long strands of hair, she paused, wondering what could have possibly made Ayla so terrified.

"Honey," Ayla's mother said, "what happened? What are you afraid of? What were you dreaming about?"

Ayla heard her mother's words, but her mind was still elsewhere. It felt like she was in between reality and the dream. She couldn't understand what it meant, why it was happening, or why it had felt so real. *I could almost touch her,* Ayla thought, remembering how she had tried one last time to reach for the girl and realized she did not possess any fingers on her hands to clasp hold of. That thought made Ayla shudder again and close her eyes trying to erase the image from her memory.

She held onto her mother for a few moments just like she had as a small child. It felt good, though she was not about to admit it. But, nevertheless, it was a comfort and a relief. She was instantly calmed, though still puzzled. She knew it had only been a dream, but unlike any dream she had ever had, this felt like she truly had an out-of-body experience. She remembered feeling the warmth and her own fear, the smell of the dilapidated old house, and sensing the dread she had seen in the unknown girl's eyes.

Ayla's mother began to feel her daughter's body soften, her breathing become relaxed and even, and she breathed a sigh of relief. She herself was exhausted and wanted both of them to get a good night's sleep. Instinctively, Ayla spoke softly and quickly, "Mom, you can go on back to bed; I'm okay now." As she said those words, Ayla did not necessarily feel them, but she was completely awake and realized that her mother had probably gotten in late and was very tired.

She felt sorry that her mother had even woken up to tend to her. Ayla again implied that she was okay, and her mother left her with a hug as she turned the light off. "Whatever is going on or troubling you, please just tell me, Ayla. I'm here if you want to talk." Her mother's tone of voice was evidence of her concern, but Ayla did not reply. She didn't want to. There were too many unanswered questions right now. She needed some time to think.

Ayla sat back in the bed and pulled the covers around her. She tried to close her eyes, but the recent images kept flooding her thoughts as if her very mind were seared with their impression. Even if she wanted to go to sleep, the thoughts kept replaying themselves in her mind, so vivid and unsettling. Ayla tried to think of other things, happier things, but nothing changed her thoughts. After a few minutes, she sat up in the bed and reached out to grab some of her recent test papers from her book sack.

She turned on the small lamp on her nightstand and it immediately illuminated areas of her bedroom. Its light cast small shadows on portions of the wall and, for a moment, Ayla felt like they were dancing upon the wall in defiance. She shook her head and pulled her knees up to her.

As she sat, she began to study the topics that she knew Mr. Curtis would discuss in her history class. It had always been a subject she enjoyed. It fascinated her and she had always excelled in it. Just the facts and her notes made her mind refocus on reality. In it, she found comfort and reason. Ayla studied each and every sentence, dozing off and on until once again the first rays of sunlight drifted in and she pulled the covers off and stepped out of bed rather tiredly.

Glancing at the clock, which also sat on her nightstand, she gasped, realized she was going to have to hurry a little bit more this morning. It was also the day of the pep rally, so Ayla dressed quickly and packed her cheerleading outfit and pom-poms into her book sack along with her books and notebook. She stuffed the loose notes she had studied the night before into one of the sections rather absentmindedly as she tried to remember everything and head downstairs.

The weather was overcast, so she grabbed a light jacket from the closet, headed up the stairs, and grabbed a small muffin as she opened the door and yelled out to her sister. "Hey, Sis, wait for me!" Ayla called out, still trying to run, hold the muffin, and put her book sack onto her shoulder at the same time.

Ayla's sister looked around and chuckled, "Ayla, what's up? Trying to get your beauty sleep?"

Ayla narrowed her eyes, "I wish, Sis. Actually, I didn't get much sleep, so I'm feeling pretty lousy."

"What happened, you okay?" Ayla's sister shot back as she stepped first onto the steps of the waiting bus.

"It's a long story, and I'm not really sure if even I understand what I'm talking about, so maybe when I figure it out, I'll talk to you about it. I think it's safe to say I had a really, really bad dream and I am glad it's over," Ayla commented back and stepped onto the bus as well.

The worn school bus was alive with chatter as students walked down the aisle to find a place to sit. Old homework papers littered the spaces on the ground between the rows, and Ayla steered toward a clean and quiet seat, but in the end it proved a bit difficult. So instead of searching further, Ayla resolved to take a seat next to a young boy who was a couple of grades higher than she.

"Hi," Ayla said, trying to brush a few wisps of hair out of her eyes. The boy looked up momentarily but did not reply. Ayla felt her face redden, suddenly feeling a sense of embarrassment as if maybe he thought she had sounded stupid or something. It was too late at that point to get up and move if he did, so she sat there until they reached school, trying her best to keep her back toward the boy who did not answer her. Once the bus had finally made a complete stop, Ayla sighed and sat quietly while the older high-school kids bumped, joked, and prodded one another as they exited the bus first. Then the bus driver began speaking into the intercom again to remind everyone else to exit the bus in a single line.

Ayla sighed again and stared out at the school. The weather was still overcast and looked forlorn to her. In fact, it seemed to cast shadows against the school's dark brown bricks, making it look almost intimidating.

Wish I were still in bed, Ayla thought, trying to stay awake but having difficulty. Already her eyes wanted to close due to her lack of sleep the night before. "Stay awake," Ayla said to herself and stood up on the bus, making it a few steps forward before feeling a tug on her left shoulder. Ayla whipped around only to see her little sister laughing at her.

"Hey, Ayla," she called out. "Earth to Ayla, where are you?"

Ayla tried to smile back, but she knew it was going to be a long, long day. "I'm here," she echoed back to her little sister, "I just don't wanna be."

Ayla exited last, making sure her other siblings had gotten off the bus, and pulled her backpack up again over her shoulder. It always kept slipping off and was both an annoying and constant struggle to keep it in place. But today, Ayla was almost too tired to notice it. She was more performing the motions than anything. The wind had started to pick up, and Ayla felt rain against her cheek. Maybe only a few drops here and there, but definitely enough for Ayla to pick up her pace as she hurried to her first class.

She glanced down at her watch and entered the north side of the building. The hall was almost empty, and Ayla again glanced at her watch. Either she was a little early for the next class or late for her current one. Walking even faster now, she neared her second class. As she opened the door, Ayla felt it being pushed toward her. She almost lost her balance but steadied herself when she realized it was Ms. Cooper on the other side of the door.

"Oh, good morning, Ms. Cooper," Ayla stammered, trying to regain her composure. Ms. Cooper's dark, beady eyes stared back at her through her horn-rimmed spectacles. Her face contorted from a frown into a smile and then into a frown again.

"Oh hello, Ayla," Ms. Cooper said in a low, raspy voice, eyeing Ayla up and down as she spoke, "glad somebody's ready to take my algebra test; you're the first one here."

Ayla gulped. *That's today?* This was horrible; she hadn't even studied.

Ms. Cooper studied the expression on Ayla's face and then let go of the door. Ayla slowly walked on into the classroom and to her assigned desk. Ayla could feel the tension already and her body began to sweat. She hated math and knew that if she had any intention of passing, she should have studied. *Too late now*, she mused. Nothing to do but give it her best. The algebra test was lengthy, and Ayla took her time to answer each question thoroughly.

The rest of the day proved to be less stressful, though she continued to force herself to stay alert. After school, the bus drove them home and she completed her normal routine of supervising everyone's homework and finishing her chores. She fell asleep rather quickly and, oddly enough, did not dream at all.

Chapter 4

The Town Sheriff

Sheriff Taylor sat quietly in his patrol car eating a couple of bran muffins and sipping slowly at a hot coffee that sat upright in the leather console. His tired eyes skimmed over the local newspaper and the weather forecast for the rest of the week. Nothing really seemed out of the ordinary, and he tossed it into the empty passenger seat. The papers rattled and landed haphazardly, of which the sheriff took no notice. He took another long sip of his coffee and yawned. The steam from the coffee escaped from the small lid opening and into the air. Its smell was pungent, yet sweet, and the sheriff smiled to himself as he inhaled the aroma, still thinking of something amusing one of the deputies had said earlier when he arrived at work.

"Such amusing young fellows these days," he pondered and glanced up at the rearview mirror, only to reveal eyes that had seen too much and a face weathered from lack of sleep due to nightmares. *What was that?* He struggled to remember what his wife would always say. Something about letting the past go and looking toward a brighter and happier future. But thoughts of old tragedies kept flooding his mind, leaving him to grimace and continue to sip his coffee.

Sheriff John Taylor was in his midforties but had always tried to take care of himself, at least from a physical standpoint. Both he and his wife had always tried to educate most of their friends and family about healthier living, but it had mainly fallen on deaf ears or perhaps just stubborn ones. The majority of the town lacked the sophistication to make changes regarding their lifestyles and most, if not all, had been raised in a day where everything was fried, fatty, and salty, so Sheriff Taylor, despite his coaxing, relied solely on his wife to support his beliefs. Every now and then, they would enjoy food at the local diner. This was the South, after all.

Most of the deputies were young newlyweds who, despite their own beliefs, had seen very little action with their time on the force. In fact, other than Charlie, who was a bit older than Sheriff Taylor, he was the only one who had stayed after the incident. Most of the previous force, some of which had been Sheriff Taylor's longtime friends, had not been able to stomach it after that and found other positions. Charlie, whose keen eyes never missed a thing . . . Charlie, who, no matter how vicious the crime scene, did no more than grimace, save that one.

Although he had stayed with the force after that, Sheriff Taylor had caught a tear or two in his eye during the closure of the case and pretended not to notice.

Heck, Charlie would've denied it anyway. Maybe time really does heal some wounds. But even now, no one talked about it. Not friends, not family, not even the town. It was like either everyone still felt disbelief and sadness, or worse, they felt a sense of embarrassment for not having done something when it was happening, before it was too late. Sheriff Taylor tried to block out the images, but they always came back.

Even so, years later, it felt like just yesterday. He closed his tired eyes while he sipped at his coffee again. There the images were again— her walking with her little brother and sister in happier times, her eyes smiling back. He winced at the image. She had always been intelligent and friendly. An image flashed in his mind of her as he recalled a couple of articles in the local newspaper owned by a nice gentleman who had always chosen to dedicate at least two or three pages each week to the local children's accomplishments. Sheriff Taylor tried to block out more pictures of her in happier times, but they would simply resurface moments later. *Had she been abused even then?* It was hard to think about. He tried to blink and have another sip of coffee, but this time another image appeared. One not so friendly, one that had haunted him for all these years since then. His wife had often comforted him when he would wake up shaking from the images, but even she could do little to truly ease his mind.

Initially, the department had offered a psychologist to come and speak with all those who had witnessed or worked the case. The sheriff had refused.

Yes, he had met with the psychologist later on and said enough to pass her little evaluation, just like everyone else. Whenever there was a murder, everyone on the force had to be evaluated, so it was nothing new. He had known all the right things to say—easy answers for easy questions. Problem was, he really had been shaken up by this one. In his time as a law enforcement official, he had seen at least six murders, but only one like this. Everything else had been things such as bar fights, petty thefts, or drug deals gone bad. Nothing like this. Maybe a little wound or a gunshot. But overall, simple. Never this vengeful, never this calculated. Never a child until then.

Sheriff Taylor twisted in his seat. The leather felt stiff and uncomfortable. Trying to readjust himself, he switched the seat a little further back from the steering wheel and again took a sip of the coffee. It was still warm and relaxed him for a minute. He could already feel the nerves in his back burning and tingling. Whenever he thought of things like that, he would tense up considerably and his back would ache from it for days afterward.

"Try not to think, try not to think," he chided himself. But it was uncontrollable. The image that he was ultimately dreading finally materialized—the lifeless nude body of a young girl. Tall, skinny, black and blue. Eyes open, staring into oblivion. Her hair was matted to her scalp with bits of leaves and twigs in between the strands of her hair. Her tongue protruded in a bulbous mass with the tinged bruise marks clearly on her lifeless neck. The smell was gut-wrenching, almost unbearable. The sheriff closed his eyes even tighter, remembering the stench.

Charlie had spied her body first, both of them not really knowing what to expect when his office had first gotten the call regarding a possible casualty. The old, dusty road had been a bit difficult to find because it was so close to the bayou and full of long reeds. Charlie had exited the patrol car first with his flashlight and called out that he thought he had seen something. The sheriff recalled his own footsteps in the dark as he turned around and inched closer and closer to the river bed.

They had both stepped out of the patrol car knowing that was their only option. It was too close to chance getting stuck out there in the mud and the muck. Charlie had chosen to walk in front while the sheriff had trailed a little further behind, glancing to and fro for any signs of foul play or anything amiss. The gnats had been especially bad that spring and out there near the water, just like the mosquitoes, they multiplied quickly and in vast numbers. For a minute, he and Charlie had walked quietly, slowly, trying to pay attention with all their senses, and then the smell hit their nostrils almost simultaneously. It could not be mistaken for anything other than human death. It was then that Charlie had stopped, not even looking back, just eyes transfixed as he eyed the lifeless corpse that lay in the overgrown thicket. Little did they realize, it was only the beginning of the gruesome scene.

A bare foot, which jutted out awkwardly, led to the rest of the nude and badly beaten body. At first, due to swelling of the skin and discoloration on the face, it had been difficult to make a positive ID, except to say that it was definitely a young female.

Unlike the other murders, even touching the body would be out of the question until they could alert the forensic pathologist and the crime-scene unit (CSU) located about fifty miles from town. The sheriff was reminded of his call to Gladys, the dispatcher, telling her that the CSU needed to be contacted immediately. "It's bad, real bad, Gladys," he had said into the phone. "We need them and we need them now."

Charlie, who never followed protocol, had already pulled some blue plastic gloves from his pockets and rolled the small body over to see if anything else could be deduced. Only then did they notice the true extent of the pure viciousness of such a horrible crime. The head appeared to be swollen tremendously on the left side toward the temple, a very obvious sign of blunt-force trauma. The face's discoloration due to strangulation grew more apparent by the marks to the neck and extended muscles. The chest and rib cage were extremely thin and bruised due to malnutrition and prolonged exposure to physical abuse. The stomach and pelvic region appeared almost prepubescent due to lack of proper nutrition. The legs were badly bruised and mangled as if there had been attempts to break them. The arms were also bruised with the hands tapering into balls of mangled flesh from the fingers being severed from each hand. The lack of blood loss was indicative of them being severed after death.

Charlie had pointed quietly to each as Sheriff Taylor nodded. Charlie had done a prelim on the body with his pocket recorder and had begun pushing the matted hair away from the face to get a better look. It was clear already that this was a very thin and tall girl, approximately fourteen to fifteen years of age who, by the look of it, thankfully had suffered much of the abuse to the body postmortem. As the hair began to fall away from the face, they gasped. Both Charlie and Sheriff Taylor recognized her as the missing girl, Meg Flander. Only this time, the face they recognized stared back with expressionless eyes and the mouth forever frozen in a gasp for breath, grotesquely misshapen due to the protruding tongue.

Sheriff Taylor awoke with a start, not realizing he had slipped off into another daydream. For a while, the visions had subsided. But these days, they had started to come and go randomly as if he could not control them anymore. *Can't let them know,* he thought, trying to take a quick sip of the remaining coffee. It was cold now, and he leaned out of the patrol car to spit it out onto the sidewalk, when he glanced up to see Ayla skipping down the street and entering a small shop on Main Street. Sheriff Taylor's heart stopped for a moment. It was like seeing a ghost. Had he seen right? She looked so much like little Meg, and yet the clothes were clearly from the city. *Maybe she belongs to that new family that moved here not long ago.* "Boy," he said, "I feel sorry for her" as he looked to see some people turn away from her direction. *It's terribly uncanny.* His mind began racing as he wondered perhaps if she was the cause of the reoccurrence of his visions. Maybe he had seen this young girl somewhere, and it subconsciously had affected him in some way.

He needed to talk to his wife. Maybe he could see a psychologist in the city. Yes, that would be okay. Keep things like that out of the local gossip. Lucy, his wife, would understand. She always had. Sometimes though, he would never admit it; his wife and his faith were really what held him together. After that incident, the whole town had become tight-lipped. Guilt spread like wildfire and there was enough to go around.

The sheriff had butted heads with the media when they had tried to investigate the department, all trying to point fingers, lay blame, and generally cause a circus right before trial. It had been a fiasco and since then the whole town had resolved to be silent, as if it did not exist. Many state officials had been fired due to the disregard of protocol and faulty procedures, which had indirectly led to Meg's death. Lucy had been there the whole time, holding his hand, reminding him that it would soon be over. And for a few years, it wasn't so bad, maybe one or two nightmares a month, until now. It was starting to become uncontrollable like it had been in the beginning.

Sheriff Taylor put his seat belt back on and started his patrol car. An announcement about a possible domestic abuse situation had just come across the radio, so it was time to get his mind out of the past and back to the present. He put the patrol car into drive and slowly meandered away from the parking place. He announced over the dispatch that he would personally head out and see what the disturbance was about. Like most, he hated calls like this. However, usually, the sight of a patrol car would impart a little sense into the people who were arguing and typically would resolve the issues peaceably. Nobody liked to go to jail.

He arrived at the location of the call about fifteen minutes later, actually, not far from where they had discovered Meg's body. It was an old, worn, decrepit mobile home. The skirting underneath it was bare in some parts, and the rest hung like broken hinges, all bent and muddy from the last rain that had left almost two inches a couple of days ago. *Great*, Sheriff Taylor thought sarcastically, *my shoes are gonna be full of mud.*

He stepped out and was about to curse under his breath when the screen door to the trailer opened with a jolt. A woman with her hair all in a mess called out loudly, "Sheriff, it's over; he's gone. I told him not to come back."

Sheriff Taylor could hear a child crying in the background. He instinctively looked around for any signs of the man she spoke of. It appeared empty in the yard, at least of vehicles. He must have peeled out in a hurry, leaving the woman and child with no way to get help.

"What a jerk," he muttered under his breath. He walked quickly toward the trailer and onto the uneven porch attached to it.

The woman could not have been older than thirty but looked as worn as the home in which she lived. The sheriff could see that she was going to have a shiner on her left eye, though it was only beginning the first stages of swelling and discoloration. He did however notice that the other eye was also discolored, yellowish in color, evidence that she had been beaten not long ago. Had she called the law for that incident as well? He was pretty sure that this had been his first time to this home, but maybe some of the other officers had come here. Why had she even let him back, and where was the child that he was sure he heard moments ago? "Ma'am, I'd like to come in if I may," Sheriff Taylor said matter-of-factly, figuring while on call it would be best to make sure that everything was really okay and that there was no immediate danger present.

"Oh . . . okay, Sheriff, I told you though, Bobby Lee's already gone now. We're fine."

"I know, I know, just wanna talk to you for a minute; it won't take long." The woman seemed nervous, peering into the eyes of the sheriff and then past him toward the road and patrol car.

"Are you afraid, Miss Christine?" He waited briefly for her to speak.

"No, not really," she said hesitantly. "It's over now. He's probably seen you here and skedaddled for good."

"Okay, Miss Christine, like I said earlier, all I wanna do is come in and talk with you for a minute."

Christine knew that the interaction was unavoidable and replied sourly, "Well, okay, but it can't be too long. I got to get my boy washed up and fed."

Sheriff Taylor nodded and stepped inside. It smelt dank and sweaty. Old beer cans littered the kitchen counter along with ashtrays completely full of every different size of cigarette butt. The couch appeared to be olive in color but was torn and tattered from either years of use or neglect. A mound of spilt Cheerios lay on the floor next to it where a small cat also resided, and the smell of feces and pet odor was pungent. The sheriff felt his stomach churning, but his composure remained intact.

"Well, Sheriff, are you gonna take a seat?" the woman said as she studied his face.

"Uh . . . no thanks, I'm fine," he replied. "I'm so used to sitting, it's nice to just stand," he continued, trying to make a valid excuse for not sitting on the couch.

Before the sheriff began to ask his questions, he heard another whimper. "Ma'am, is that your boy here with you?"

"Yes, Sheriff, I have a four-year-old. He gets fussy sometimes, 'specially after he hears a commotion. Bobby Lee never did like his crying like that; he says it makes him angry. He was never one to have any patience." The sheriff nodded apologetically as if to convey sympathy but really only to hide the churning in his stomach. *How can a mother allow herself and her child to live in such squalor?* he thought.

"So, what's your son's name, Christine?" Sheriff Taylor asked, once again snapping in and out of thought.

"Levi," she replied flatly. "'Course, Bobby Lee never did take a liking to that neither," she added with a bit of emphasis.

"Well, now, Levi is a fine name. Kinda like the sound of that myself. Ain't too common, kinda catchy." The sheriff smiled and motioned for the woman to fetch the young child from one of the darkened rooms and bring him out. She seemed reluctant, although from the sounds of the child, he was in need of attention. When the woman reappeared, she held a tiny, thin boy in her hands, straddling him on one hip as if he were still a baby.

The sheriff glanced down at the little boy. He was skinny and small for his age. His hair looked like spun gold and his eyes a deep brown. His eyes were swollen around the lids as if he had been crying for quite some time, and his underwear hung loosely from the heaviness of urine. In fact, the smell of it had immediately permeated the entire room with its nauseous odor. He wore no clothes, only the underwear, and looked hungry and scared. The sheriff was not pleased. "Ma'am, is there adequate food and clothing for this child? Seems to look neglected to me," he retorted angrily. The woman squinted her eyes at the sheriff.

"Just what do you mean, he looks neglected? I thought you wanted to come in and talk about Bobby Lee and what the heck he did to my face, not tell me that I ain't no good momma."

"That's not what I said, ma'am," Sheriff Taylor quickly replied. "I just can see that his underwear looks like it hasn't been changed for a while, and only God knows how long he's been crying in there. I did come to get information about the incident before writing my report; however, it's also my job to make sure everyone is all right and assess the situation, which is what I'm trying to do."

The woman still looked offended, but said nothing. Perhaps intimidated, perhaps not. The small boy began to squirm and wiggle in his mother's arms so she let out a long *humph* and let him down. He instantly squealed with excitement as if he had been cooped up in one of those rooms.

"Do you mind if I look around?" he said.

"I guess, but there really ain't nothing to see. Fact of the matter, Sheriff, is me and Bobby Lee fight all the time. Don't know why we still together, probably cause he threatens me and I believe him. Once I seen him put a pistol to a man's head down in Charleston and ever since then, I believed him. Told me he'd kill me if I left him."

"And you really believe him?" the sheriff asked.

"Oh, yes, even when I get mad and we fight and he leaves, I always end up letting him come back in. Sometimes he pretends to be nice and tell me he's had some time to think about things, and other times he comes home drunker than when he left and keeps slapping on me."

The sheriff pulled his pen out again and looked up at her as he wrote in his small notebook. "When you say 'slap,' what do you mean? Literally, or he hits you with a closed fist or object?"

The woman paused. "He's hit me every which way you can imagine. He even put a cigarette out on me once. That hurt worse than you can imagine," she said, stating this fact as if it were an old war story. "He's even hit little Levi a couple of times, but he's all right. I heard once that kids his age can't remember nothing." The sheriff stood back almost in shock. Had he heard correctly?

This woman was admitting to abuse in this home and showed such little emotion that it was startling. In fact, it was almost a normal thing and a sense of accomplishment to her. As if it made her stronger to have survived these fights.

Sheriff Taylor jotted more of her conversation on the paper he had in his hand and bent down to see the child. The boy put up a valiant front, but his eyes gave him away. They were sad, frightened, and wounded. "Hi, little fellow," Sheriff Taylor said as he extended his hand. The sight of his badge glistened and glimmered, attracting the young boy's attention, though he said nothing.

"He don't talk to strangers, Sheriff," the woman said, and picked him up again. "Besides, I think I've answered all your questions. I'll see you to the door."

Sheriff Taylor knew that was his cue to leave and walked quietly to the door and out to his patrol car. Once inside, he turned on its ignition and heard the familiar sound of its engine. Slowly, he eased the car out of the muddy driveway and back onto the old gravel road that led to the outskirts of town.

Twenty minutes later, he finally arrived back at the station. Getting out of the car, he thought about the small boy. *Just like Meg.* A helpless innocent soul lost among the strains of society and all alone. *What has the world become?* he thought, inwardly feeling profoundly saddened at the answer he already knew.

Sheriff Taylor walked into his office and shut the door behind him. Rubbing his hands across the back of his neck, trying to ease the tension, he picked up the phone and dialed the number. A woman's voice said hello.

"Hi, hon," he replied quickly into the receiver. "Need you to make some phone calls and inquire about any outreach programs for victims of domestic abuse for adults and children. I'm headed home in a bit. I love you."

Chapter 5

Lucy

Lucy had been Sheriff Taylor's wife for twenty-six years, a task that was as hard as it sounds. And despite his status, she went to bed and awoke each morning with just as much stress, if not more than he. She constantly worried for his health and safety, though through the years she had felt her faith and hope strengthened by attending church regularly and helping out at a local charity dedicated to children.

Their marriage had been strained a bit ever since they had discovered that poor girl's body. Things had taken a turn for the worse. First, it had been the shock, then the grief, then the guilt, and lastly the reoccurring nightmares that would awaken them both from much-needed rest. Lucy had suggested many times that he should seek counseling about it, even offering to go with him. But she had heard word that he had refused when the department initially offered, so it did no good to keep pressing the matter, though she secretly wished he would confide in her. It had been tough trying to comfort him when she didn't know what he was really feeling. Perhaps he felt as if it would hurt her, she tried to reason. It had changed their lives dramatically and, for a time, had made him so withdrawn that she had ended up seeking the help of a counselor for her own feelings of helplessness.

Some of it had been therapeutic, some not so much. In fact, it was only when she had decided one Sunday to pick up a worn and dusty

Bible and head to the church she had been raised attending that she really began to see a difference. It had been awhile since she had attended, but ever since that day, she found more peace through its doors than anywhere else. Initially, it had been just her attending and leaving her husband behind. But lately, he had attended church with her, giving her a hope that things were starting to improve.

Lucy glanced up from her thoughts and checked the clock. It was time to start making dinner. John would be home soon, and so she began to quietly gather the ingredients for dinner and set each of them onto the countertop. As she began her preparation, she once again drifted to the past. John had always wanted to be sheriff of Tate County. He had been twenty-two then—a young deputy with a dream. He had attended every seminar and finished every academy assignment at the top of his class. His IQ was considerably above average, and he was the most physically fit of any of the other deputies. Actually, anyone on the force for that matter. A fact he had boasted about for a long, long time back when things like that mattered to him. She recalled their first date and how he had shown up at her parents' doorstep in his uniform. How glad she felt now that she had opted to hold her tongue from either laughing at him or scolding him for wearing his "work clothes" on their first date.

Only after years of marriage was it revealed to her just how sensitive and how passionate about his job he really was. It was more than a job, more than just filing reports, it was his life. "His calling," as he had referred to it so many times. Lucy had simply nodded through the years trying to empathize as much as possible. Though she had to admit, it had not always been easy. In fact, sometimes it had been extremely difficult. The election itself had been taxing on everyone and when the final count was revealed, she was not the only one who had breathed a tired sigh of relief. Both had given so much to their careers, realizing early on in the marriage that they could not have children. Lucy recalled his face when the doctor had come back into the examination room with the disappointing news that she could not conceive. They both held one another quietly sobbing, but grateful that they still had each other. It had been a very sad time, as both of them had truly wished for a child, but every time she had offered lectures or donated time at the community center, she felt connected enough to soften the blow of knowing that she could never experience the joys of being a mother. It was a task she relished now more than ever, though she had always regretted not being a part of the center before the murder. How tragic.

Her thoughts began to swirl around those horrific events. The facts, the situation, and the inevitable damage it had done to the community—how damaging it had been to her husband. He still woke up with nightmares and cold sweats. It had been years, but it felt like days. For a while, they had lessened, become more infrequent, and then, as if the years had meant nothing, they began again. *Why?* she pondered. Hadn't the media and everyone else done enough blaming, exposure, and overall damage to the stability and sanity of everyone's nerves? It had all been so taxing on her husband, causing her to feel angered still. Yet, in another way, she knew that due to its atrocity and exposure, many things had significantly changed in the town and the state regarding abuse. For that, some much-needed light had been shed on such tragedy and a deeper understanding as to the urgency of change.

Though she knew that many more children needed help, each day that she went and volunteered time, the looks upon the children's faces was of hope and not of despair, as if their small voices had now been heard. Now, if only her husband and the rest of the town could come to terms with the past, they could possibly flourish again and move to happier times.

As she closed her eyes in deep thought, she heard the front door open and the steady footsteps of her husband in the doorway.

"Dinner's almost ready, honey," she said, managing a smile of encouragement.

"Hmmm," John sighed, "smells good," and he started walking toward the oven to see what was making such a delicious aroma.

"Hey, now," Lucy playfully called out, "wait your turn. It'll be ready soon enough." Lucy managed to put her arms around him and guided him toward the living room to sit. The TV was already on, and voices from the news anchors could be heard in the background. Sheriff Taylor glanced at it and sighed loudly. The news was featuring a breaking story of a wanted fugitive in connection to a burglary and murder in one of the neighboring towns. "Oh, great, just our luck, another creep on the loose." She positioned herself in front of the TV so that he could not see the rest of the story, sat him on the couch, and propped his feet up to allow him to sit back.

"Whatever would I do without you, Lucy?" Sheriff said and cupped her hand in his. The gesture was innocent and yet held her heart for the moment. How she worried for him and hoped that soon enough his health would improve and that the nightmares would fade away for good. She smiled over at him and let her hand linger.

"I could say the same about you too. This ain't a one-way street," she stammered and laughed. He smiled back, though tiredly, and positioned a small pillow behind his back to alleviate some of the tension. It had been a long day and his head was throbbing.

"Glad you're just letting me take a load off," he said and put his hand to his head. "I needed this; trust me." She turned around and looked down at him lovingly. Even after all the years and the effects of both stress and age, she still thought he was the most wonderful man she had ever known. Had it already been twenty plus years of marriage? Funny, he still gave her butterflies.

"Well," she said laughingly, "looks like I didn't have much of a choice; it was either have you snooping in the kitchen to see what was for dinner or motion you toward the couch."

His eyes were closed, but he managed another weary smile. She was glad at least for that and walked back into the kitchen to tend to the finishing touches for their usual feast. Meatloaf had always been one of John's favorites and with a pot of hot mashed potatoes, you couldn't ask for more. There was nothing like down home Southern cooking. The smell of fresh, hot dinner rolls permeated from the kitchen and into the living room and brought him slowly back into the kitchen.

Lucy quickly took her apron off and set the table, bringing each dish of food one at a time to the table where she liked them.

"You feel like talking a bit more now?" she asked as he heaped generous portions of the mashed potatoes onto his empty plate.

"Not really," he shrugged. "Sometimes it's better to just enjoy a little silence."

She tried to smile at him, but it was difficult. It had been so hard through the years after the incident for him to open up at all inwardly.

She blamed a lot of that on his stubborn pride and the burden of guilt he continued to carry, though it was not his burden to bear.

The meal was finished with a few sighs, pauses, and a few comments made by Lucy describing her day and what she might do for the rest of the week with her at-risk children's programs. He knew how much she enjoyed her time with the children, but he did not always wholeheartedly agree. His thoughts began to drift away as his eyes tried to remain focused on hers. He began to think of *her*, always *her*. Her lifeless eyes. How frail, how forgotten. Why did it always seem like she was calling to him? She would visit him in his dreams, always taking him to strange places. Dark places, repulsive places, and then she would reach for him and he would shudder or scream. He could feel the pressure in his chest when she would come to him, the coldness that felt as if it seeped into his very bones and the thought that he would never be rid of it. Lucy could see that he was not with her though his eyes remained transfixed. "Honey, are you listening to me or on another planet?"

She was trying to lighten the mood, but it did little to change his demeanor. He blinked his eyes and apologized. "I'm sorry," he said. "It's like it has gotten worse in these past months. Like she's alive, but not really. I don't know what it is, but it's always like she's trying to tell me something, something I'm supposed to figure out, but never can."

"Hey," Lucy said. "I read a book somewhere about something similar to that. I believe there were very different situations regarding the death, but I remember that the father kept seeing the child long after the death. They did some kind of study because they thought he was having hallucinations or something, but each time they would test him, he would reveal something he had learned. I remember thinking how sad and how interesting at the same time. Whether or not I want to truly believe any of this, I have resolved myself to be objective. If not, you and I are both going to go crazy. And I can't have that, at least not any time soon. If something can be revealed in these horrific dreams or will ultimately help her find peace or whatever and allow you to have a normal life, then so be it. I'll start keeping a dream journal for you, and maybe we can both try to make sense of all of this." As she spoke, she reached and grabbed his hand, squeezing just enough to let him know that whatever happened, she would be there.

He looked forlorn but managed another sheepish smile and squeezed her hand back as if in agreement. "Sure, hon," he said. "I'll try." He let go of her hand, gingerly standing up and pushing away from the table.

"Oh, no, you don't," she said, watching him begin to pick up their dirty dishes. "I've got that. You already never get a moment's rest."

"You know, I'm not an invalid; I do know how to clean up after myself," he said softly back.

She smiled at him and handed him her dish. "Okay, then," she said, "just thought that I should be tending to you." As she looked up, he had already put their dishes into the sink and was heading to the living room to sit on the couch.

Lucy picked up the rest of the food and utensils from the table and cleaned up the kitchen before joining him. An old western was playing on the television, and the plot was an obvious one—looters had managed to rob a stagecoach only to come into a town that abided by the law and had a sheriff willing to do anything to uphold it. It was sweet and yet bitter. It seemed to her that all the old westerns seemed to only point out that no matter how good things could be for people, how many opportunities there were to do and be anything, there would always be those who would sooner cut your throat to get ahead than earn an honest living. *Not much changes.* She sighed. The crime in their town was not as bad as some of the neighboring towns, but there was still some and there was no need for it. Domestic abuse, petty theft, drunk driving, and then of course the murder that had shocked their entire community and left her husband a shell of a man.

She looked down at the couch, instantly realizing that the faint sounds of snoring echoing upward was from her husband as he had once again drifted to sleep from sheer exhaustion. She moved around the couch and pressed the button to turn the television off. She then set the remote back down on the wooden coffee table and sat on a small space on the couch next to him. She began to slowly stroke the hairs away from his forehead, looking intently at his furrowed brows and troubled face. Even in sleep, he could not find peace. She continued to take her fingers and lightly rub them against his temples and down his cheeks. His face softened a bit as if his body was responding to her touch. She smiled to herself and continued to rub his face.

She continued to do this until finally she felt the muscles in her arms beginning to ache. "John, wake up, so we can head to bed." The sheriff lay there motionless. "C'mon, hon," she called out again. "You're gonna feel so bad if I let you sleep right here through the night." As she spoke to him, she tugged ever so gently but firmly on his hand.

His eyes slowly fluttered and looked at her sleepily. "What's the matter?" he said groggily.

"Nothing," she said. "It's just time for bed, and you've dozed off again on the couch. You're gonna get a cramp in your neck and feel horrible. Besides, you know I can't sleep without you."

His eyes started to close again as if his lids were heavy, and his body too comfortable to be responsive. She tugged a bit harder, and his eyes fluttered open again as he grabbed her hand in his and attempted to get up. She put her arm around his waist and walked with him into the bedroom, pulling down the sheets as he lay down and lifting the covers around him. She walked to the other side of the bed and quietly took off her jewelry, except her wedding band, and walked into their spacious bathroom. She took a quick glance in the mirror and took her clothes off. Her eyes looked unapprovingly at the image staring back at her, and she stepped back with a shrug. Walking to the large tub, she turned the hot water on and grabbed the towel hanging on the rack adjacent to the tub. She also grabbed her book of crossword puzzles along with the pen. For some reason, she had always reveled in the quiet time she had as she took her bath. Whether it was to finish a crossword or one of her devotionals, it brought a sense of relaxation to her. Sometimes when she would be at the center, she would comment to the other staff that this was the only therapy she required. They, of course, would laugh in disbelief because it was so simple.

The water was nice and hot, just the way she liked, and she slid underneath the bubbles, allowing herself to drift away if only but for a moment. The house was so quiet, not even the stirring of covers pierced the silence, though she knew he was already asleep. She pulled her hands out of the hot sudsy water and dried them off with a small hand towel that was draped slightly over the edge of the whirlpool tub. Once dried, she grabbed the crossword puzzle and pen that she had already set on the adjacent edge of the tub and began to read and write her answers. Lucy scanned the questions and quickly wrote down the answers, though a few made her pause and recall something deep in her mind that she had either remembered from another completed puzzle or she had read or seen somewhere. Before long, the crossword puzzle was completed, and she put the book back down on the side of the tub and began to wash herself.

She took the washcloth, poured some of her favorite soap on it, and worked it into a rich lather beginning with her face, down her arms and torso, her legs were next, and finally her feet. She smiled with all the suds. Something about this had always fascinated her as a child; it made her feel like a princess getting ready for the ball. She let the water begin to drain and turned the faucet back on to rinse the remaining suds from her body. She then took the shampoo and conditioner from the shelf by the tub and began to wash her hair. Once finished, she rinsed herself off thoroughly and stepped out of the tub. The warm, plush towel draped around her petite frame like a blanket. Again, she tried to not be so critical about herself, but it was hard, and again she looked into the mirror disapprovingly, although her fears and critical nature of herself were unwarranted. In fact, she still was quite stunning, but she would have never believed it.

She put her pajamas on quickly and picked up the dirty clothes to take downstairs to the laundry room. Sometimes, John would take a shower at the police station, so she didn't seem alarmed when he simply dozed off earlier. "Probably took one there," she said quickly to herself.

With that, she marched down to the laundry room and emptied the clothes into a small hamper parallel to the washer. Turning off the overhead light, she walked back up the stairs and lifted the blankets of the bed, sliding underneath them with a small but well-deserved sigh. Her pillow felt plush and comforting against the back of her head. As she dozed off, she put her arm around him quietly, yet tenderly nudging her face to his back and fell asleep.

Chapter 6

Back on Mrs. Tilly's Porch

Back on the porch at Mrs. Tilly's, Ayla once again sat with eager anticipation as Mrs. Tilly began to recollect old yet precious memories of her youth and the like.

It would almost always begin once Mrs. Tilly had been poured a cold glass of sweet tea that was loaded to the brim with lemons. Then she would promptly sit in her favorite rocker and begin to rock ever so gently against the wind. Ayla, on the other hand, enjoyed the sun on her face and would always position herself seated against one of the columns on Mrs. Tilly's steps.

"Well now," Mrs. Tilly began, a sign that she had gotten comfortable.

"Some things have been on my mind lately, and I'd like to talk to you about it. Just don't think I'm strange, all right?" Her eyes stared across the porch and bored into Ayla's for a sign of a response. When Ayla looked back at her quizzically, Mrs. Tilly shrugged her shoulders and heaved a deep sigh. Ayla smiled to herself knowing Mrs. Tilly always did that before she began a long talk. Looking up at Mrs. Tilly, she sipped some more of her tea and waited.

"Well, first things first. Has anyone ever told you that you resemble someone who used to live here?" Ayla shook her head. "Guess I'm kinda surprised that nobody has talked to you about her," Mrs. Tilly said, looking at Ayla intently.

"Who, that girl who used to visit you?" Ayla answered back.

Mrs. Tilly shook her head as her hands shook a bit. The ice in Mrs. Tilly's tea clinked against the inside of the glass, and she paused to stop her hands from shaking before she spoke again. "Well, you weren't here yet, dear. Just thought somebody would've mentioned something to you by now . . . well, since you look just like her."

"I really don't know what you mean," Ayla began to say, but inside her mind a rush of dread slowly filled her mind as she thought back to the strange dream of the girl with no fingers. The one who kept calling out to her, the one who kept flooding her dreams.

Mrs. Tilly put down the tea for a moment and looked even more intently at Ayla. "Well, if what you say is true and you really don't have any inklin' of what I'm speaking about, then I feel like you had better hear it from me, before anyone else muddles the truth up!"

Ayla nodded in agreement but still tried figuring out what Mrs. Tilly meant.

As she picked up her tea again, Mrs. Tilly began. "See, it all started a long, long time ago, 'fore anyone really knew what was going on. She was beautiful, tall, skinny, but the saddest eyes you ever did see. Child, those eyes were so sad it made ya' wanna cry when you saw her, but for what none know. She was smart like you, kind, but very, very quiet. I use to let her come when she could, and she would sit right where you are and listen to me ramble. There were times where I would start to ask her why she looked so sad all the time, with no light in her eyes, but I never did. I regret that now, you know. But back then, I figured she'd talk when she was ready."

Mrs. Tilly stopped for a moment before speaking again as if she had gone deep into her own thoughts unaware that Ayla was hanging on every word. Ayla tried to be patient but was starting to become aggravated at Mrs. Tilly's tendencies to drift off before finishing her sentences.

"Anyhow, where was I?" Mrs. Tilly said and eyed Ayla.

"About the girl's forlorn eyes and wishing to ask her why they were so sad," Ayla said.

"Oh, yeah," Mrs. Tilly replied, never apologizing. "The day it all happened I recall getting up and feeling different. It was a regular ole day—hot, sweaty and sticky—but something in my mind just told me something was different, and I couldn't shake the feeling. So I did my usual things and tinkered around in the garden waiting for her to get off the school bus and sit a while with me while I reminisced about something funny from the past, but she didn't show. I had made a big old pitcher of iced tea but drank about half of it myself waiting, and then went on inside the house figuring she must have had some chores or something to do. I went to bed not much later, but I still couldn't shake that same feeling that I'd had earlier that morning."

Ayla looked at Mrs. Tilly's hands, noticing that they were trembling once again. "It's okay, Mrs. Tilly, you don't have to tell me anything that is upsetting; we can wait another time or something." Ayla started to get up from where she had been sitting.

"No, child," Mrs. Tilly said with a whisper, "I feel the need to tell somebody."

Ayla sat back down and once again Mrs. Tilly relaxed her hands and spoke.

"You see, honey, the gnawing feeling I had that day is cuz something really was wrong; I just didn't know it at the time. Most of us didn't anyways, 'cept Sheriff Taylor and ole Deputy Charlie. They knew and I'm guessing it was the worst day of their lives."

"What, Mrs. Tilly, what?" Ayla drew a deep breath trying to coax more from Mrs. Tilly before she drifted away again.

"She was murdered," Mrs. Tilly spoke in almost a whisper as she looked at Ayla. "I tell ya, it's such an awful shame. That poor girl didn't deserve to die like that."

Ayla sat quietly for a moment, not sure what Mrs. Tilly was going to say next and not sure if she really wanted to know. Even the air around her in the hot sun seemed to get colder, and Ayla could feel the goose bumps starting to rise on her arms.

"It was Sheriff Taylor and the deputy that found her. She had never made it to school, and the principal had been suspicious. Meg always had perfect attendance, always straight A's. It just wasn't like her to not be there for school, so he had called to see about her. By that time, the sheriff's office had gotten a call from her mother claiming that Meg had gone off missing, and she didn't know where she was. The sheriff had already visited that home a few times for domestic problems in the past and knew the family. So, he and Deputy Charlie went out there to get a statement from her mother and any neighbors who might have seen or heard something. But they say when they got there, he knew something wasn't right with her mother's story so he brought her to the station to talk to her some more. That's when he sent the rest of his deputies out to look for Meg, but nobody could find her. Since she initially refused a lawyer, they were able to question her and within a few hours, she finally confessed to killing her and where she had dumped the body. Can you believe that, a mother harming her own child? I tell you that ain't Christian," Mrs. Tilly said matter-of-factly.

"Well, they found her all right in a part of that nasty marshland not far from the house, without a single stitch of clothes. Oh, it just makes me wanna cry, thinking of it!" Mrs. Tilly exclaimed.

Ayla sat still, afraid to move for fear Mrs. Tilly would wander off with her daydreaming again and forget to finish the story. Her glass of iced tea was still almost full, though most of the ice had now melted, vanishing into the sweet copper-colored drink.

"Why would her mother do something like that?" Ayla asked, looking aghast.

"Well," Mrs. Tilly began, "her mother was a mean woman, heartless to the core. She had always been jealous of Meg. Never the other children, mind you, just her. The child services and Sheriff Taylor already had been out there on a few occasions cuz of the way she treated little Meg, but child services never did nothing about it. Knowing they could've saved that little girl's life and didn't was a terrible, terrible thing. From what I gather after the sheriff found her, he ain't been the same since, but no one confronts him. It was a big to do, you know, small town like this. Why, even the big city papers got wind of it and for a long time that's all you would read. When the trial finally happened, Judge Leonard had to bar most of those reporters from getting in and making a circus outta the whole thing.

"Can't even imagine how Meg's father and siblings felt while all that was going on. But after a while, the jury finally convicted her, and she was sent up the river to some special jail where it's for only women who commit murder and stuff like that."

Ayla sat dumbfounded, thinking of her recent nightmare. *Is this the same girl? It couldn't be, could it? Why was she in my dreams? What does she want? Is there more to the story than Mrs. Tilly knows?* Ayla's thoughts flooded her mind, but she pushed them back and looked up at Mrs. Tilly. "Mrs. Tilly, nobody's told me that story or anything like that since we moved here. Most people just look at me and my family like we came from outer space or something. Unfriendly like, but they don't even know us. You're really one of the few people since we moved here who has made it a point to say hello. I mean, my dad meets some of the people when he needs to represent them, but other than you, we were kinda unsure about our move here," Ayla said forlornly.

"Don't feel so bad about all that. Most people around here buttoned up after she died and haven't talked about it or how it changed this town. Not to mention the fact that you look a lot like her. I mean, you could have been a sister for sure. The resemblance is amazing." Mrs. Tilly just shook her head as she spoke almost in disbelief. Ayla wondered about all those stares the townsfolk gave her and if it was because the girl had looked just like her. She stared down at the small watch on her left wrist. It had been a couple of hours now on Mrs. Tilly's porch, and the sun was starting to set.

"I'd better head home now, Mrs. Tilly," Ayla said as she stood up and dusted off her shorts. She walked up toward Mrs. Tilly and brought the half-empty glass to the small side table that sat by the rocking chair and wrapped her arms around Mrs. Tilly. Mrs. Tilly softened her shoulders and extended her arms around Ayla. The action was almost perfunctory in the Deep South but not insincere. Ayla had always had a soft spot for Mrs. Tilly and enjoyed their afternoons together. It was more like therapy for both of them and a peaceful oasis from all the chores at home.

Ayla's dad had questioned her about Mrs. Tilly when she had first come to visit, but resolved that if Mrs. Tilly really enjoyed Ayla's company, who was he to refuse? Ayla had always been tenderhearted and compassionate. Her nature had always been one to tend to others, so in all honesty, Ayla's father wasn't too surprised at all the time she visited with Mrs. Tilly. Maybe it was good; the lady probably was lonely he had reasoned.

Ayla began helping Mrs. Tilly grab the tray with the glasses and the pitcher that sat next to them. As usual, she would help Mrs. Tilly gather everything and bring it into her kitchen and offer to help her clean them and put them away.

"No, no," Mrs. Tilly said and smiled feebly, "gives me something to do," and she chuckled almost apologetically.

"Okay," Ayla said, "but I'm offering, just in case you change your mind." Ayla backed away from the kitchen sink and walked to the doorway. She had almost gotten to the front door when she noticed a small wooden frame that needed quite a bit of dusting. Ayla wasn't sure why she had noticed it among all the other trinkets and frames that lay cluttered about, but for some reason she was drawn to it and instinctively reached out to dust it off to see the picture it contained. She paused, realizing it may have some sentimental value to Mrs. Tilly and stepped away from the frame. *Another time*, Ayla thought and walked out the front door and onto the porch. A small breeze brushed its way against Ayla's face, and she inhaled the fresh air, feeling energized.

"Well, I'm off, Mrs. Tilly," Ayla called back, and slipped down the front of the porch and onto the road home.

Ayla skipped for quite a distance and then walked as briskly as she could the rest of the way home. It had occurred to her that her father might not look too favorably at how late it was again for her to be coming home. Ayla knew her father relied on her to have dinner made, the house cleaned, and to oversee all the other children's homework. It was a formidable task with so many siblings, but when Ayla's mother had opted to return to college late in life, the tasks had now fallen upon her. *It's not so bad, just a lot to remember.* She enjoyed feeling so needed and happy that her mother had followed her pursuits.

Sometimes, it would be well after the other lights turned off that Ayla would pull her old backpack out and go over her homework. She could have probably done it much sooner if she didn't visit with Mrs. Tilly, but she enjoyed her time listening to Mrs. Tilly and wouldn't have traded it for the world.

Ayla finally arrived home. She walked down the long and dusty driveway of her parents' home and into the house. Ayla's dad was in the kitchen with a concerned look on his face. "Ayla, have you been at Mrs. Tilly's?"

"Yes," Ayla replied, looking a bit sheepishly as she spoke.

"That's fine; I just need for you to let me know what days you are going to visit and when you are coming home sooner. I was just about to start supper and was getting a bit worried."

Ayla looked at her father. He looked tired and a bit disappointed. She knew he was under a lot of stress with his work. Even on family vacations, he always managed to sneak his laptop into his suitcase, much to the chagrin of her mother. "Vacation is vacation," her mother used to always say. But then she would smile and give everyone a hug. Guess she knew how he was and that he would never quit working. No sense in trying to change that. Best to just make sure what time they did have together was good instead of bickering.

Ayla nodded to her father and gently grabbed the vermicelli out of her father's hands. She set it near the oven and pulled out two very large pots from underneath the stove. The ground beef was already sitting atop the counter adjacent to the stove, so she took it and put into one of the large pots, sprinkled some seasonings on it, and turned the knob on the right side of stove to adjust the heat. Next, she put water in the other pot, set it on one of the other burners, and adjusted another large knob to allow it to boil before putting the vermicelli inside to cook. Her mind was elsewhere as she worked, but she shrugged off the eerie feelings about what Mrs. Tilly had told her today. It couldn't possibly have anything to do with the strange dreams she was having, or could it?

"Ayla!" her dad yelled, looking at her oddly. "Where are you? You look like you're lost in outer space over there."

Ayla looked up, having broken her stream of thought, and shrugged, "I'm here. Just thinking about something Mrs. Tilly had said to me today. You know how she is, one minute making sense and the other who knows."

Her dad nodded as if he knew exactly what she meant, but did not say a word. From the sound of clatter, all her siblings had completed their homework and were slowly making their way to the kitchen. Ayla was sure they had realized she had made it home and was making their favorite dish—spaghetti.

"Hey, Sis," they all chimed in, gathering close to her, eager to eat. Ayla had originally felt slightly overwhelmed when her mother had left the majority of the household responsibilities to her. It had been a bit tough, as she had initially seen a drop in her grades due to the changes, but then finally it just became routine. During the summer, things weren't so time consuming and hurried. Ayla could get in a few hours to take her brothers and sister down to the lake, which was not far from their house, or on a hiking trip through the woods to do her 4-H projects. But during school it was different. All homework had to be completed, the house straightened, the baths taken, and dinner well on its way. *Sometimes,* Ayla thought, *there isn't enough time in the day to complete everything,* but then quickly realized her mother had done it for years.

Maybe that's one of the reasons she liked Mrs. Tilly's talks so much. It was just her and Mrs. Tilly. No one to watch, no hurried chores, no responsibilities, just good conversation and delicious sweet tea.

The water in the large pot began to boil. Ayla took the vermicelli and broke it in half, letting it fall into the boiling pot. She then took a couple of teaspoons of olive oil and poured it into the steaming water. Next, she stirred the meat browning in the neighboring pot and added the spaghetti sauce and some more seasonings. Now all she had to do was watch over it while she put a load of laundry in the wash and set the table. There was so much she had never realized her mom had done each and every day to take care of them and keep the house in order.

Man, this is tough, Ayla thought. She hadn't even begun to work on her own homework, and she had a hard test the following day. Most of Ayla's teachers were nice and understanding but not the one for her science class. She was tough. No nonsense, no excuses. You either had your homework done and good test grades or you didn't. *What happened to grading on the curve?* The clothes in the dirty clothes hamper smelled like sweat, and as Ayla reached in to grab them with one hand, she held her nose with the other. "Yuck," she said aloud, though no one noticed. After the clothes were in the washing machine, she adjusted the switch to allow the water to run over the clothes, and then she put the laundry detergent in. Adding an additional scoop of detergent wouldn't hurt anyone, and she smiled as she dropped another capful of blue liquid into the machine. Ayla ran back to the sink to wash her hands and stir the sauce again.

The vermicelli looked soft, so she took the colander out from another cabinet, poured the pot's contents into it, and let it sit in the empty sink while she grabbed the plates and silverware to hurry and set the table.

"Hey!" Ayla called out, "dinner should be ready in about thirty." No one replied, but Ayla wasn't surprised. Normally, nothing happened until the food was actually ready, and then it was a flurry of hungry children coming out of nowhere and descending upon the kitchen in a frenzy. Soon, Ayla would quietly slip away as everyone was eating, and finish her bath and homework before returning upstairs to clean up the kitchen, make sure everyone had finished his or her homework, and were snug in their beds.

Ayla's father had decided to use part of the three-story house to keep as his office, and though it was difficult to move to such a small and wary town, he had made every effort to visit with the townsfolk and show up every Sunday at one of the local churches, sometimes staying after the sermon was over, just to make an effort to say hello and make them comfortable about a new lawyer from the "big city" coming to their neck of the woods. It wasn't easy at first, Ayla recalled. Most of the people still stared at her kinda funny, but when she began staring back, they stopped doing it as much. Ayla had just attributed it to "country folk" and their superstitions and misgivings about strangers, but sometimes it had felt like it was something else, something more. But just what, Ayla did not know. All she knew was that her feelings didn't matter one way or another at the end of the day. This was where her mother and her father needed to be, and they would adapt, even if it was a bit painful.

After everyone had eaten as usual, Ayla returned to assess the damage. Plates were littered about along with half-full glasses of fruit punch. *What a mess*, she thought, but began picking them up one by one until after about an hour, she had cleaned up and washed everything in the sink. Once again, the kitchen looked presentable. A lone plate full of food was stuffed in the microwave for her mother when she returned. Ayla smiled, thinking that one day she would have a family of her own. As she walked down the stairs, she realized that she may have to forego visits with Mrs. Tilly for a while, at least until she could find more time to do what she needed to do. She opened the door of her small bedroom and grabbed the book sack that lay by the bed. Once she was finished with her homework, she lay down and closed her eyes, still recalling the odd dream she had experienced a couple of nights before and hoping that maybe she would never have to worry about thinking of that awful dream again. But she was wrong. As Ayla drifted to sleep, the same girl continued to reappear, looking forlorn, desperate, and determined to tell her story to Ayla. Despite shutting her eyes tighter, nothing could block the thoughts running through her mind.

Chapter 7

The Fight

Little Levi sat in the corner shivering and shaking; his dad and mom were fighting again. At the very back of the large and worn sofa, Levi had managed to find a small crevice where he would hide when they would argue. He could always tell when it would start. His father would start by throwing the empty bottles in the living room at the walls, splashing old contents and glass about the room. Ever since he had been cut once by a piece of glass from one of the bottles, Levi had done his best to hide out and stay away until his dad was gone. It made him so afraid sometimes that he would urinate on himself, and then cry as he called out for his mom. The arguments would never last for more than a few minutes, but they seemed like an eternity to Levi. Why did Mommy always let him come back in?

Levi's beautiful eyes looked sad and old already. A product of seeing more than one should, but none had ever thought to question it. The police officers would come and speak to his mother and, as always, she would remain cold and aloof, promising them that she would never let him back in, but as usual moments later, sometimes even hours, he would bang on the door with some more bottles to drink and an even angrier tone in his voice.

"Bobby Lee," Christine snapped. "I really can't take your crap anymore. I told that sheriff that you was gonna have to leave this time, and I mean it . . . every word." Levi crouched further into the crevice, though his little ears strained to hear again. He could tell that his dad was very drunk now because all he seemed to do was stumble to each and every room of the trailer, mumbling things that he couldn't understand. Levi knew this time it was really bad, but every time he got upset, his mommy would tell him that his dad was going to get help soon and that he needed to be her big boy. But the days had turned into weeks and the weeks into months, and soon Levi realized that his mommy was wrong. Daddy would never change, and she needed help too.

"Bobby Lee, I'm talking to you," she said again, this time more direct in her tone. "We can't keep living like this. You gotta get that help you said you was gonna get." Bobby Lee just stumbled again, this time crashing against a small table that stood in the hallway near the bedrooms. His hair, matted and greasy, his clothes dirty and unkempt, his eyes half open, though the look was maniacal.

"Woman, this is my house," he said, slurring and looking at her with disgust. "I oughta break your friggin' nose for ever talking to me like you run things around here."

Christine still stood but backed a few feet away.

"What, you don't like that, you filthy whore?" Bobby Lee sneered. "Where's my little brat of a son anyways?" When she did not reply, Bobby Lee spoke again as he wobbled and tried to balance himself so he could stand. "Probably took that li'l cuss to your sister's house, huh?"

Christine did not reply, she just stared at him as if lost in translation or maybe stunned. Levi could barely make out her silhouette as he peered out just far enough to glimpse but still remained hidden.

"Bobby Lee, you know that's not right how you're talking to me," she said, softly this time as if she were afraid.

Bobby Lee continued to balance himself all the while sneering at her and making strange noises. Christine backed up a bit further, this time keeping at least three feet between them. Bobby Lee noticed her backing up, this time letting his smile turn into a cruel grin. "Scared of me, ain't you? Well, you should be. I told you last time that you weren't gonna get away with calling the cops on me again. I warned ya and ya didn't listen." Bobby Lee spoke even steadier and finally balanced himself, though his right hand continued to hold on to the moldy wall for support. His voice was harsh, and she knew he meant it. He was gonna hurt her again. She cursed at herself now for having called the sheriff, but she was so scared that if she didn't tell on Bobby Lee, child services would get involved, and then she would lose Levi forever. Even the bruises or bloody noses wouldn't matter. She couldn't bear to lose Levi. He was her little knight in shining armor. *Mommy's big boy*, she thought, and smiled quietly within.

Why did Levi have to have a father like this? She was always so scared, thinking that if they got in the old truck and packed up their things that Bobby Lee would find them and punish them for leaving. She couldn't count the times he had threatened to really punish both of them if they left him. She could hear his threats echo in her mind again and again as she tried to stand firm in the hallway with him looking menacingly at her. Why had she stayed for so long? Was she now just as crazy? She could remember a time when the boys would whistle at her as she crossed the road, a day when her hair would glisten in the sun and her skin was beautiful and glowing. Memories long tucked away since she had met Bobby Lee. He had come to town and talked so sweetly to her years ago that she had forgotten anything else. He was rude and crude, and yet he used to open the door for her and buy her roses for Valentine's Day. Now all he brought were punches and cases and cases of his favorite beer. She had given everything and everyone up who had mattered in her life for him.

He had kept her from going to her friends or family for support, constantly cursing them for his feelings of inadequacy and always making her feel that if she told anyone, she didn't really love him.

When she had been at her lowest point, Levi was her salvation. The day she had gotten up as usual to look at how badly Bobby Lee had blackened her eye, something felt different, and she headed for the toilet instead of the mirror. For months after that, she had been very doting to Bobby Lee in the hopes she wouldn't get tossed around or beaten. She had even considered going to that abortion clinic about eighty miles away, but the longer she thought of such a beautiful and innocent life, she couldn't part with it. That baby would bring life back to her, or at least she thought it would. One night in a drunken rage, Bobby Lee had raised his hand to hit her, and she blurted out about the baby. Bobby Lee had first accused her of sleeping around, but soon acted as if he were the happiest father who had ever lived. He had softened up for a while after that, and everyone had prayed that he really changed. But it was short lived. After Levi was born, he had quit his job in the lumber yard and began drinking again at a local bar with his rowdy friends. Guess they saw what was going on and agreed with him, or were too scared to cross him, because nobody but the law ever did anything about it. Everything went back to the late nights, fights, drinking, and carousing with his old coworkers from the lumberyard.

Their little trailer had been a wedding gift from her father. He hadn't condoned the marriage one bit, and he had eyed Bobby Lee enough to know that he was no good for his daughter, but the trailer was all he could afford to give them as a wedding gift, having been on disability for a leg amputation in the Vietnam War. Bobby Lee had made sure to trash it though, just for the fun of it. Just to show her he could and nobody could stop him. Christine's father and family had pleaded with her over the years to get away, but she remained scared that he would find her and Levi, or worse, come after her family and hurt them in order to find out where she had run to. She felt that there was no hope.

She knew as they were arguing, Levi had hidden in the place he thought no one knew about. She continued to keep the knowledge that she knew about the hiding place from him for fear that it would break his little heart since he had found the special place all by himself, and it was there that he would go when he was afraid or nervous.

She knew he could probably see them in the hallway but hoped that he would remain hidden until Bobby Lee left. Maybe Bobby Lee would just drink one too many one day and not come home. Then she and Levi could go outside once again, let the wind blow through their hair, and run in the green grass, unfettered by fear. Once again, she would hear Levi's infectious laugh instead of his never-ending tears. For so long, she bit her tongue and tried to look past all the hurt and pain, but the years had made her old and cynical. Maybe she could talk to her sister when she went into town for bread and milk and finally get her and Levi anywhere but here. Levi had gotten to the point of crying even in his sleep, and the noise would wake her. As Bobby Lee would roll over in the bed, she would put Levi beside her in the bed and cry with him quietly as she held him close.

Christine was jolted back into the situation at hand with a slow but still hard blow from Bobby Lee. "Wake up, stupid," he said, laughing as she grabbed her jaw. Her mind was reeling from the shock. Maybe he wasn't that drunk after all. She purposely avoided looking up at him and curled herself into a fetal position as she lay on the floor. "What's the problem, you can't talk, so now you got nothin' to say?" Bobby Lee was almost on top of her, coaxing and teasing her to look up at him so he could hit her again, but she did not move a muscle. He was still slurring but no longer holding on to the wall. She knew that the rage would soon be over.

He never took longer that fifteen or twenty minutes to use her as a punching bag and then as usual, he would leave to go drinking with his friends while she tended to cleaning up the mess and console Levi, who now understood what was going on but remained helpless to change it. *It's all my fault*, she thought as Bobby Lee pushed her hands away from her face and began hitting her repeatedly.

Levi could see and hear his mother. What he saw was gruesome. His father looked like a monster hovering over her defenseless body. He could hear his father panting as he continued to swing his fists in the direction of his mother's face. She used to show him pictures of her as a cheerleader or playing in one of the talent shows they had for her school. At first, Levi had not recognized the pretty girl staring back at him. "You looked so beautiful, Mommy," Levi had said once she told him that was really her. He crouched into a little ball and continued to stare out at the horrific scene before him. Something in him pleaded to run out and bite his father's fingers to protect his mother, but he was too scared to move. *Mommy always told me to hide from Daddy*, Levi thought. *She wouldn't be happy if I didn't*. So, Levi stayed put.

The minutes felt like hours and Levi was starting to get uncomfortable in his little hiding spot. While his legs began to get restless and his little tummy rumbled, he knew better than to move until he heard the front door slam and the sound of Daddy's old pickup truck leaving in a cloud of dust. So far, Levi hadn't heard that yet. Just a lot of rustling about and the sounds of something in Mommy and Daddy's bedroom that he couldn't define a few minutes earlier. Something quiet—too quiet. Normally, when something like that would happen, Levi's mom would wait until after his dad had left and call out for him to tell him that it was over and that he could come out of his hiding place. Then they would make a game out of cleaning the house up, and she would make him his favorite treat of ice cream with Hershey's chocolate on it. She used to tell him that he should dream about the house he really wanted and then tell her all about it. But Levi hadn't told her, hadn't said that all he ever really wanted was for her to be happy and to spend time with him.

The noise of his daddy's old truck returned, and Levi once more pushed as far as he could to the tip of the couch to see if he could get a better look. The only thing he could see was that the place where his mother had been lying was now bare floor. She was gone. Levi suddenly drew back. This wasn't like all the other times. Mommy should have been out now and watching Daddy drive away. Where was she? He waited and waited. Finally, Levi heard footsteps, though they were not the light pitter-patter from his mother's dainty feet, but the low, loud, clanking sound of his father, like the work boots he used to wear. Levi could hear them going up and down the hallway to the bathroom and then further past it toward Mommy and Daddy's bedroom. Back and forth, again and again.

Levi was really becoming uncomfortable now but remained behind the couch. His little legs had started to fall asleep and go numb, and he could hear his tummy growling even more fervently for something to eat.

But still, Levi did not move. All he could think about was Mommy. Levi began to doze off but awoke to the sound of the telephone ringing. He was unaware of how long he had been sleeping but instantly scolded himself for having dozed off and not waiting on Mommy. The phone continued to ring and ring until finally Levi heard the footsteps of his father once more. This time they seemed slower, more forceful. Levi could smell something and could see that his father had one of his cans in his hand. Levi watched him quietly as he stumbled to the kitchen, nearly knocking over the chair and reaching for the phone on the wall.

"Hello," the voice was slow and thick.

"Bobby Lee," the voice said forcefully. "Where is my sister? I need to speak with her."

Bobby Lee coughed and regained his composure. "Well, now, Laurie, I don't know. She just up and left earlier and said we was outta milk," his voice breaking as he spoke. "She didn't tell me when she'd be back, so that's all I can say about that." As he spoke, he licked his lips again, centered the opening of the can to his mouth, and took another quiet gulp as the receiver pressed hard against his ear.

"Bobby Lee, I don't know what's going on over there, but something just don't seem to be right, and I really wanna talk to my sister, so don't be getting drunk and forgetting to tell her to call me, you hear?"

"Whatever you say, Laurie," Bobby Lee slurred sarcastically into the phone and hung up. Bobby Lee could still hear her cackling voice on the other end of the receiver as he hung up, but he didn't care. *I never liked that Bible-thumping witch anyhow,* he thought, and snickered. Soon he wouldn't have to bother with this stupid town anyway. He had quietly pocketed small amounts of cash from Christine's purse for the last year and had managed to collect in a small beer can about a thousand dollars. It was enough to get to the city and take a flight to Mexico. There he could drink as much as he wanted and assume a new identity.

Everything was working out just as he had planned.

Christine had been wrong about him, and she had paid for it. If only she had kept her stupid mouth shut, but she didn't, and now he was free. Through the years, he had grown to truly hate her nagging, her attempts to get him to find a job or attend that stupid church she constantly raved about. Her whole family had hounded him for years about it and he hated them for it.

Nobody's gonna tell me what to do. He took another long gulp of beer and looked around. Even the house disgusted him and anything that brought up old memories of her.

She was always collecting old cards and gifts he had bought her when they had first met. He recalled having to stomach all of that until the wedding. It had been hard to maintain the smile. The pretenses, the family outings . . . it was if he had been caged in a body he did not recognize. He had known he could easily persuade her the minute he had laid eyes on her. She was young and naive. It had been too easy when he'd come to town.

It was like fate when he had seen her and she looked at him. But now, she had used up her worth, and it was time to move on. His rage could no longer be held at bay.

He had thought about taking Levi, but that would only slow him down. Besides, that was the last thing he needed, and it was sure to get him caught. He figured he'd have at least two to three days before someone might show up and put everyone on alert. With no one around, no one would be the wiser until he was far gone and drinking as much as he wanted somewhere across the border. Bobby Lee laughed maniacally and plopped himself down at the table. A piece of paper sat on the tattered tablecloth. It was a small drawing of two stick figures with the words "Mommy" and "me." Bobby Lee stared at it intently, and then he sneered at it as he began to tear it vehemently with both hands and dropped the pieces onto the floor.

Levi could see him very well and his little body shuddered as he continued to watch. Suddenly, the phone rang again. Bobby Lee let it ring loudly a few more times, then grabbed it violently off the wall and mumbled once again into the receiver, "Hello."

"Bobby Lee, don't you dare hang up on me. I told you I wanted to talk to my sister and little Levi. I know it's almost Levi's birthday, and I haven't see him in ages. I want to come by and bring him his gift." Laurie's voice was harsh.

Laurie had never trusted Bobby Lee. He had always treated her sister and Levi poorly, and she couldn't trust a single word that ever came out of his mouth. She could hear the phone go quiet on the other end and only the faint sound of Bobby Lee's breathing. "Bobby Lee? Bobby Lee?" Laurie called out again.

"Laurie," Bobby Lee's voice became sickening sweet. "Are you saying Levi isn't over there with you? Christine had told me that he was staying over there with you." Bobby Lee steadied his voice as he spoke, hoping that Laurie would believe his little lie and provide more information of Levi's whereabouts. He hadn't seen him since his return and figured that he and Christine had been the only ones in the house. Now, despite his current state, deep down in the pit of his stomach, he felt something different—fear. Had Levi seen anything? Was he in the house?

Bobby Lee cold hardly contain his nerves. His fingers trembled while he tried to steady the phone, his mind racing.

"No, Bobby Lee," Laurie retorted, becoming more sarcastic. "Don't you recall that you hardly let them come and visit anymore, or have you forgotten that? Maybe she took Levi with her to the store. Didn't you see them leave?" Bobby Lee put his head down. He knew Levi must be around somewhere. Christine would never have left him. He must have been hiding somewhere. He could've seen something. His plan had not been perfect. Now he would have to find Levi and eliminate the only thing that could get in the way of him and his freedom.

"No, Laurie," Bobby Lee spoke again into the receiver. "I was busy tinkering around in the backyard making something for Levi. Something he'll really like. Guess I'll have to wait until they get back," Bobby Lee said, speaking a little louder for Levi's benefit. He thought that might coax the boy out of hiding, since he seldom got gifts. If Levi would come out, he'd be able to get him to follow him outside and then into the old woodshed where he would silence him for good.

"Fine," Laurie said, not believing a bit of it. "Just have her call me so I can tell Levi 'Happy Birthday.'"

Bobby Lee hung up the phone with great ease and looked around the kitchen. Everything was still. Not a single bit of movement. He walked out of the kitchen, continuing to scan his surroundings. The house was a wreck with trash all over and lots of little nooks and crannies for Levi to hide in. He could either scare him out by being loud and rummaging through the house, or he could do this the slow and methodical way and search the entire house while calling out to him sweetly. Bobby Lee cracked a devilish smile and decided the second approach was better for now. He continued to walk through the house and down the hallway.

Levi slowed his breathing as he watched, but his heart felt like it was about to explode. He had never felt his heart beat so fast. He knew in his heart something was very wrong with Mommy and Daddy was to blame.

"Oh, Levi, Levi, where are you, boy?" Bobby Lee called sweetly, all the while looking up and down the room so he could grab him up if he saw him. But little Levi did not make a sound. He knew Daddy was lying. He knew Daddy would hurt him too if he knew where he was. Bobby Lee continued to go throughout the house calling his name or talking about the present he had made for him outside in the shed. But Levi knew better. Daddy had never made him anything. Levi crouched down some more behind the couch.

He could hear his daddy's steps become faster. He was becoming angry, and Levi knew it wouldn't be long before he tore the place apart to find him. He wanted to cry so bad and be with Mommy.

"Levi, this is Daddy, and I'm starting to get very mad now because you are disobeying me." Bobby Lee could hardly contain his rage and frustration as he began opening and closing the closet doors violently. Levi could hear things being thrown around in the other rooms and the shattering of glass as it was pushed off the shelves. Levi stared at the phone on the wall. Mommy had told him about 911.Only for emergencies, she had told him. He knew that was his only chance. If Mommy was hurt, he needed to get her some help. He still could hear his daddy throwing things about in one of the bedrooms, so he decided it was now or never.

He pushed back the side of the couch and slipped his little body out quietly. The phone was a little high, but he could reach it if he stood on his tiptoes. Levi moved as quietly as a mouse, all the while listening for the sound of his daddy's footsteps. Once in the kitchen, he tried to reach the phone, but missed it, just barely. Levi tilted his head up again and stretched his fingers out as far as they would go. He felt the bottom of the phone and pushed it off its base. The phone came down above his head and he caught it in his hands before it hit the kitchen floor. He quickly dialed the numbers and held the phone to his ear. "9-1-1, what is your emergency?" a voice said.

Levi whispered into the receiver, "Help Mommy," his voice cut short by the sound of his father's footsteps returning down the hall. He put the phone to the ground still, hearing a voice at the other end and quickly and quietly returned to his hiding place.

Bobby Lee looked around. He could have sworn he heard something, but nothing looked out of place. Then, he saw it—the phone on the ground. He raced to it and picked it up "Hello, hello," he said.

"Sir," the female voice said on the other end. "I've already dispatched a police officer to your address. He should be there shortly. Just stay on the line for me."

Chapter 8

On the Loose

Bobby Lee let the phone drop to the ground with a thud. All the color had completely drained from his face. He ran to the bedroom and grabbed the duffel bag of clothes and stash of money. He then ran out of the trailer and started the truck again.

Levi heard the truck speed away and breathed a sigh of relief. His mommy would have been proud. He darted into the bedroom and saw his mommy lying on the ground. This was not the first time he had found her lying on the floor.

Thinking she might still be asleep, he called out, "Mommy, Mommy, please wake up," while holding on to a tattered blanket with one hand and stroking his mother's face with the other. But this time her eyes did not respond, and Levi sat in the dark sobbing uncontrollably.

The sheriff stood outside the trailer as the other police officers and the old dilapidated van of the coroner pulled up alongside. Sheriff Taylor held his usual cup of coffee in his hand and tried to steady himself. His thoughts were swirling inside his mind as he recalled the last time he had spoken with Christine. He knew there had been trouble brewing for some time, but helpless to do much until she asked. Now, it was too late, and he was sick about it. He recalled the little boy with his sad eyes and distant stare. It had been hard to leave that day he had spoken with her. Now, he knew the reason he had feared leaving.

Deputy Mark Hunter had arrived first on the scene, as he had responded to the 911 call. The dispatcher had not given much information other than the caller had sounded like a small child. Deputy Hunter had noted to the sheriff that he had arrived approximately fifteen minutes after being dispatched and that no other vehicle than his had been on the premises. He had scanned the property for anything suspicious, walked up the small porch steps, and knocked on the trailer door.

He would have continued to knock, but noticed it was unlocked, and he called out in the darkness, "Sheriff's department . . . Deputy Hunter. Is everyone okay?" He had continued to walk quietly with his gun drawn, just as a precaution. They had dealings in the past with Bobby Lee, and he could be a mean SOB when he was drinking. There was no answer, but he heard faint crying in the back of the trailer.

As the deputy spoke into the intercom attached to his vest, he remained calm and continued to scan the area. "Responding to 911 call approximately seventeen minutes ago to the address of 111 Tyler Road. Caller minor child residing with mother, Christine Putnam, and Bobby Lee Putnam. No vehicle on premises upon arrival. Knocked on residence, no reply. Entered said residence in search of victims. Voice noted in bedroom down hall, proceeding to investigate, Deputy Hunter out."

Deputy Hunter walked further down the hallway and smelled a strong odor. Then the smell hit his nostrils, and he knew it the minute he had caught a whiff of it. Blood.

He continued to remain calm and pushed back the door of the bedroom. It was dark and filthy, like an animal had gotten loose. He quickly tried to adjust his eyes, but it wasn't easy. He held his gun out into the dark with his right hand and began to feel against the wall in search of a light switch with his left. Once he found the switch, he flipped it and stared down in horror. A little boy lay next to a woman of approximately 110 pounds with long hair. Her face was black and blue with multiple lacerations including an extremely large gash to the side of her forehead. Blood had pooled underneath her and continued flowing, spanning a radius of approximately three feet. Deputy Hunter also noticed a large amount of blood spatter on the adjacent wall and cringed. Neither the small child or woman was moving. He moved in closer and noticed the eyes of the woman were open, staring into nothingness. He had gone to school with her and closed his eyes as if to pay what little respect he could to her now. He fought back tears as he looked down on them both. So fragile they both looked. He could see another large gash, this one directly over the jugular and immediately knew the cause of death was not the vicious blows to her head but her throat had been cut, and the blood now trickled slowly out of the opening.

Well, he thought, *that would explain the large amounts of blood spatter,* and he instantly felt nauseous. He moved around her lifeless body, being careful not to disturb anything until the sheriff and coroner could assess the situation.

He could see no signs of physical harm or injury on the small boy and moved in closer to look. He thought he was still breathing and put his hand out as he pressed against the little boy's shoulder. Levi looked up and screamed. "Don't hurt me; don't hurt Mommy!" Levi continued to scream.

Deputy Hunter put the black 9-mm. handgun back into his holster and breathed a sigh of relief. "I'm not here to hurt you, kid. I'm here to protect you. Were you the one who called 911?" Levi studied his face, still scared.

Deputy Mark Hunter was rotund and a bit clumsy, but he had always been a favorite with the children at the police functions. His eyes were large and kind and everybody said he looked like a big kid. Levi waited for a moment and then spoke quietly, "What's wrong with Mommy? Why won't she answer me?" Deputy Hunter had no reply, watching the young boy speak as he glanced back to study the face of his dead mother.

Deputy Hunter swallowed hard. "I think it's about time you grabbed my hand and come with me. We're gonna let somebody come and see about your momma." He tried to steady his voice, but it was hard. He could feel the lump in his throat and his mouth was instantly dry as he spoke. *Poor kid,* he thought. This was the kind of thing that made him want to leave the force, things that haunted the sheriff and now him. He closed his eyes for a second, blinked quickly while he watched his footing, and extended his stubby hand to the little boy.

Levi just stared at him for a second and then brought his hand up in compliance. He did not want to leave Mommy, but he had no choice.

He knew it was bad and did not have the words to explain how he felt. Maybe a doctor could help her and they could get away from Daddy for good. The deputy grasped Levi's hand further, lifted him up and over the trash and garbage scattered about, and walked down the hall way toward the door. Little Levi looked back one last time and felt a tear run down his face as he buried his head down into the warm chest of Deputy Hunter. The sun caught him by surprise, and Levi ducked his head further, suddenly feeling very shy without his mommy to comfort him.

There were so many faces and cars. Levi studied the faces for a moment and rested his eyes on a familiar one. He remembered the sheriff coming to his house and speaking to his mommy. He knew that he had tried to help him and Mommy. Instinctively, Sheriff Taylor looked up from the paperwork handed to him and locked eyes with the troubled boy. Inside his head, he could almost hear the little boy's silent pleas for answers, though he knew he could not say. The little boy would no doubt have to attend some form of counseling prior to being given to other family members.

What a sad shame, Sheriff Taylor thought as he put his head back down and began reading the papers in his hands. Though the coroner would need to provide him with an actual report for the file, he could review some preliminary notes and proceed on his end based on those findings. Everyone already knew it was Bobby Lee, but he knew he needed to have that confirmed.

Two of the deputies searched the yard and gathered information from the tire tracks for make and model of Bobby Lee's vehicle as well as noting whether or not that was the only vehicle in the proximity of the house. It was an undertaking to say the least. Trash and various broken objects littered the entire yard. *It is impossible to fathom that these people have lived in such disarray for so long*, the sheriff thought. He could feel his heart growing heavy as he tried to not become impassioned with the case. It had always been hard for him. Senseless death was something that had always struck a chord in him and fueled the fire to exact justice on whomever was ultimately responsible.

But nothing in law enforcement was ever easy, and even Sheriff Taylor knew he had to follow protocol, no matter what the situation. The papers merely showed sketchy first impressions from the coroner.

He had ruled her death as a homicide with cause of death being a sharp object, probably a small to medium knife hitting her jugular vein in the middle of the neck, though she was badly beaten prior to death and lost enough blood to warrant unconsciousness. He prayed that she had in fact been unconscious at the time of death, but more thorough testing would be done to make a full report once they had transported her body.

He could feel the tension in the air as deputies and other various employees of the state's crime lab moved back and forth around the corpse of Christine Putnam. It was going to be a serious undertaking from the looks of things, but Sheriff Taylor knew what he had to do. Every second Bobby Lee was not behind bars was a very serious problem. He needed the coroner to put a rush on this and let him pursue Bobby Lee with a court order. *Time is always your greatest enemy*, he thought and felt a cold chill run up his spine.

Unlike the other, Bobby Lee had not stuck around and pretended to be unaware of the incident. The sheriff knew that Bobby Lee would be trying to flee the country if he could and that if they didn't watch out, they would lose him forever.

"Hey, Walter," Sheriff Taylor called out to the coroner. "Can I talk to you for a minute?"

The coroner glanced over his shoulder and spoke with a small sigh. "Sheriff, I already know what you're gonna ask me. My report should be ready in the morning, and I'll give a call to one of my friends at the crime lab and bend his ear to move quickly."

The sheriff nodded and patted Walter on the shoulder. "Can't let him get away with it," he said quietly under his breath and walked back toward the trailer.

By the time he pulled into his driveway that evening, the day had felt like an eternity, and he welcomed the familiar smells of Lucy's cooking and the warmth of their home. The years of law enforcement had wreaked havoc on his health, both mentally and physically, so any reprieve was always welcome.

He closed his eyes and leaned his head back, resting it softly against the headrest. For a second, he sat trying to think of a happier time, but his thoughts were of the sad little boy who had stared at him so forlornly that morning. Child services had been by the sheriff's department earlier that day to discuss where he would reside and it had been a complete circus, with everyone milling about but resolving nothing. The deceased woman's next of kin were called; they were emotional to say the least. They wanted Bobby Lee brought to justice, which was not going to be a simple task. No one knew where he had gone; there were only ideas and speculations. Bobby Lee had no family here and had been very vague as to where he had really come from. Now it was going to be nearly impossible to track him down. They were going to need some serious manpower in order to conduct the search. Sheriff Taylor dreaded all the phone calls he was going to have to make in the morning, but he knew it was necessary.

Images of the little boy continued to resurface in his mind and made his heart heavy. Mrs. Putnam's sister, Laurie Richards, was going to try to care for the little boy until a decision could be made by the state's child services, but indicated out of the little boy's earshot that she already had five kids and was barely making ends meet. He cringed at the thought of the poor boy's future as a ward of the state passed around from one facility to another or worse one home to another, never fitting in, never belonging. He rubbed his forehead and grabbed his empty thermos as he stepped out of the truck. The lights were dim but still on as he walked through the door.

Setting his thermos down in the kitchen, he saw his wife coming down the stairs. He could tell from the look in her eyes she had been crying and instinctively he knew someone had called her to tell her the latest news. She had always been sensitive like that, which had always appealed to him. She was kindhearted and empathetic to people's needs. Even now, after all these years not much had changed. He met her and held her close. "Oh John, that poor, poor woman," her voice pausing as she spoke, letting the soberness of the words hang heavy in the air.

"I know, honey, God rest her soul. Hopefully she's found peace now." Sheriff Taylor continued to hold her as he spoke. "Guess you know, ole Bobby Lee has skedaddled outta town, and we gotta go track him down and figure out what's gonna happen to the li'l boy."

Lucy looked up squarely into his eyes. "What do you mean? Doesn't the little boy have any family . . . aunt, uncle, grandmother . . . something?" Her eyes looked intently at his for the answer.

"Well, the woman's sister came to the station after she was notified and gave a statement about speaking to Bobby Lee right before the . . . incident." He gulped, trying to just state the facts without emotion. "Child services or some dang reps from the state were there to discuss the little boy's current and future prospects. But it wasn't good. He can only stay for a while until they find him a place to go. The poor woman's family keeps claiming they don't make enough money to keep him. I tell ya, Lucy, it took everything I had not to tear up. The whole thing just makes me sick. Taking a mother from her child and all . . ."

Lucy held her husband close as she fought back tears. How could someone do something like this? First, that poor girl and now this woman. What had happened to their small and peaceful town? Her mind raced as she tried to form some rhyme or reason for any of this, but she could not. It was as if a horrific sadness had engulfed her and would not ease up. She knew that her husband would be forced to face the town and provide answers and, once again, he'd be bombarded by the nightmares, cold sweats, and visions of ghosts with stories that would forever remain unchanged. When she had gotten the call from Judy, Deputy Hunter's wife, she had thought she was dreaming. Judy had relayed the gruesome particulars and Lucy had been forced to sit down due to the wave of nausea she felt as Judy continued to ramble.

"Can you even imagine, Lucy?" Judy had said with dismay. "I always knew she was getting hit. I used to see her sometimes with a small boy in the grocery store, you know the one on Edward Street? Well, anyhow, I used to see her always with her head down and holding hands with that little boy. One day I recall she was at the register and the cashier had called for a price check, and she had looked up for a minute. It was then I had seen the bruise across her left eye and cheekbone. It was an ugly thing, half green, half yellow. Come to think of it, she had quite a lovely face if it hadn't been for that ugly bruising. Her eyes looked like she was looking beyond at something . . . still gives me the willies." Judy paused to catch her breath and then spoke again, "Lucy, you there? Lucy?"

Lucy had answered after a long breath, "Yes, Judy, I'm here. Just trying to think of what we should do now for the family. They must be devastated right now, especially the little boy. Why, he's got to be beside himself without his momma around."

Judy let out a long sigh and said, "Well, I don't know, but I'm sure the local paper has gotten wind of it now, and soon it'll be all anyone talks about. Just like that poor girl. I thought people would never quit talkin' about that." Judy let out a small growl as if exhausted by all the gossip she was dishing out and bit her lip waiting on Lucy's response. If left alone, Judy would do nothing but ramble.

"Judy," Lucy said quietly, "I think I'm gonna go finish that laundry I started. I'll give you a call sometime tomorrow to discuss if there has been any new developments," and before Judy could say another word, she hung up the receiver. As she did, she breathed a sigh of relief. Judy was as sweet as she could be, but she enjoyed discussing the goings-on of everyone in the town. Sometimes, this wasn't so bad if the news was pleasant, but when it was not, it felt almost uncomfortable to her. The idea of speaking so nonchalantly about others' plights had never impressed her, but as the sheriff's wife, some things were just unavoidable.

Her thoughts jolted back to the present and the warm, but tired arms of her husband wrapped around her. "Oh, honey, all I keep thinking about is that poor little boy. I wish there was something we could do." John looked down at his wife. He knew what she was thinking even before she had uttered the word—adoption. He knew that was near to impossible and, depending on the incidents prior to the death of his mother, there was sure to be some serious psychological problems. *Suffice it to say*, he thought, *this kid's gonna come with some serious baggage.* Yet as he thought of the negatives, his heart felt a connection to the little boy when he had been called out to investigate. He had looked into the boy's eyes and had seen hope. Hurt, yes, but still hope. It wasn't the poor kid's fault. Sheriff Taylor knew the boy probably never even felt love from his father. No structure, no security. Things all children should have, no matter the circumstances.

"I know what you want given our personal circumstances, dear, I just don't think that's even possible. We talked a long time ago about adopting and what it would take. It would be too hard on you to connect with a child and for us not to be considered by the adoption agency. It was best then and it's best now that we just leave things alone." As he heard himself speak, he doubted his own words. Deep down, he wanted badly to be a father, even though the years had gone by and they both had become committed to their careers. He just didn't want her to get her heart set on this and be disappointed. His stress from work alone had been hard on both of them. No need to complicate things.

"I know John," she said, looking up at him. "There's just something about that little boy . . . he needs us."

"No, you mean he needs someone *like* us," he quickly chimed in.

"That's not what I meant, and you know it. I think we can try it if you're agreeable. We are loving and financially stable. We could offer him a good education and a happy life. Promise me you'll look into it, okay?" Lucy pinched him gently and walked into the kitchen to make his plate of supper.

"Sure thing, hon," Sheriff Taylor said half-heartedly as he sat down on the couch and turned on the television.

His face dropped as he saw the headlines of every local news channel he turned to: WIFE SLAIN IN HOME, KID WATCHED. The media were already piecing together what they claimed happened. He cringed but said nothing. The news reporter had managed to interview a few local people, including Lucy's friend, Judy. He was infuriated by their lack of specific details, or rather the fact of disregarding them. *This isn't news*, he thought, *this is a media fiasco.*

Here they come again, just like the last time. Big-time executives from the city reporting what they believed was the product of hillbilly ignorance and brutality. He knew, somehow, somewhere Bobby Lee was seeing all of this and smiling to himself. The television station had managed to capture multiple shots of the residence and even released a few photos of the woman and the little boy.

Someone had let them onto the property. Sheriff Taylor felt his face burning but remained as calm as he could. As far as he knew, the crime lab and his people were still collecting evidence.

Lucy called that dinner was ready if he wanted it. "Yeah, hon," he replied. "I want it, but watching this just makes me lose my appetite. Why can't they just let us do our jobs first before trying to broadcast it to the world?"

"Don't know, but before long, I have a feeling you are going to have to deal with this just like the last time. More invasion of privacy, more media at our house and the station. Hope you and I can get through this a second time."

"Do we have a choice?" he said, grabbing the plate of warm food and nodding.

"Not really," she said, "kinda comes with the job. It's never gonna be peaceful as long as people like Bobby Lee exist." Her face twisted in a grimace as she spoke his name and a chill went down her back. She stared at the television screen for a few moments and then walked back in the kitchen to make her plate and finish cleaning up.

Chapter 9

The Chase

The next morning, Sheriff Taylor kissed his wife goodbye and headed to the station. A part of him wished it had been a Saturday morning and he could have just rolled over underneath the warm comforter and nestled closer against his wife, breathing in the scent of her hair and skin. The years had not diminished his love for her in anyway. Time might have changed their appearances somewhat, but he felt no differently. She was such a necessary constant that life would feel unbearable without her.

The station was no more than a few miles from their home, and as the sheriff turned the corner, he saw numerous vans parked outside—not a good sign. Each one was a different media source. He counted at least seven different news teams.

Just like last time, he thought as he fumed and drove up to his regular parking place. As he stepped out of his vehicle, a melee of cameras, microphones, and people seemed to appear out of nowhere. They began to push and poke one another in order to get close enough to his face.

"Sheriff, Sheriff John Taylor!" someone called out from the crowd. Sheriff Taylor looked around at the sound of his name but was unsure as to who in the sea of reporters had actually called out. He continued to make his way toward the door of the station, but it was difficult. He could feel the eyes upon him and resisted the very basic instinct of screaming back to leave well enough alone.

"Just keep walking," he said to himself.

"Yo, Sheriff," the same voice said with no distinct face in the crowd. He knew that to reply to the voice would only fuel the flame of reporters, but if he did not, he came across to the viewers watching that he was heartless, uncaring, and lacking in direction.

Sheriff Taylor paused in his tracks and turned around quickly to face them, instantly realizing that the video cameras were directly in his face. "No comment, except to say that this department and its agencies are working hard to collect all the evidence to conduct our investigation, and we would sincerely appreciate it if you would let us do our job." He turned back around and kept walking, but the same voice insistently pursued him.

"Look, while I appreciate that you all have a job to do, so do we." Sheriff Taylor's voice became firm with his back still turned away from the cameras. "This investigation is not over and when it is, you will get my statement." By that time, he was nearly at the door and breathed a sigh of relief as he opened it and quickly felt it close behind him. He was away from the commotion and on to real police work.

All eyes were on him as he continued down the corridor and toward his office. Even the dispatcher glanced up as she continued to answer the phone. Many calls had been pouring in from people who were either nosy or thought they may have seen Bobby Lee. Once inside his office, Sheriff Taylor shut the door behind him and let out a huge sigh.

Ayla's dad, James Abernathy, had not had many run-ins with Sheriff John Taylor. For the most part, he had briefly represented the city on a few protective order violations, but other than that, nothing. Having watched the news, like everyone else, he knew that sooner or later he would be receiving a phone call. It had been a struggle moving the family here initially and although most country folk were pleasant, they still had those who were untrusting of outsiders. James knew his daughter, Ayla, had especially had it hard, though he was the first to scratch his head as to why. He recalled the first time he had gone into town and Ayla had mentioned that she felt odd around the townsfolk as if they were staring at her. At first, he had laughed it off, thinking she was somewhat paranoid about moving to a new place and trying to fit in, but when she continued to complain, he started noticing that her complaints had some validity. It was as if they had a look of recognition and then withdrew from his daughter. Was it imagined? She had never done anything to anyone in town, nor did anyone know her when they first moved here. He shrugged it off to just something he couldn't explain and went on to watching more of the news.

Local stations were always great to watch, but unless you stepped in and out of the room, what you got was about three or four repeat commentaries and then it was over. Basically, the latest breaking news was a couple of minor stories that were repeated throughout the broadcast. He had seen enough and walked out of the living room and into the kitchen. As if on cue, the phone rang loudly and Ayla's dad pressed the receiver to his ear. "Mr. Abernathy," Sheriff Taylor's voice said tiredly. "You got a minute to come by the station and go over some stuff with the victim's sister? Seems there are some issues regarding all this custody garbage, and I might need your advice. What do you say, can you come by? Say maybe around 3 p.m.?"

Ayla's father sighed. "Well, I would, Sheriff, but I'm working on something today that's got a deadline. I could come by tomorrow."

"What about later today?" Sheriff Taylor replied into the receiver.

James could tell that the sheriff did not want to drag this out until tomorrow. "All right, I'll see what I can do, but I can't make it there until after four today."

"Fair enough," Sheriff Taylor said, "I'll see you then."

The local police station had not been remodeled in ages, though it had needed repairs for many years. The worn tile and the spotted ceiling from water leaks made it all the more apparent as Ayla's dad stepped through the doors and down the hallway to Sheriff Taylor's office. The smell of ammonia and bleach lingered from the cleaning crew. The halls were littered with a series of pictures. Some were of prior sheriffs and deputies who had made an impact in the community, others simply encasing old newspaper articles evidencing the state fair, various town holiday gatherings, and a few acknowledgments from local political officials. Ayla's dad walked past them all, slowly taking into account a few here and there that sparked his curiosity. It wasn't long before his footsteps became slower and slower, finally stopping at the very end of the hall. The wooden door was closed with an old name holder firmly attached, which read: Tate County Sheriff John Taylor. James Abernathy knocked on the door. When he heard footsteps heading toward the door, he quickly took a deep breath. This was not going to be pretty and he knew it. No one was going to end up completely happy, and it had already been traumatic enough for that poor child.

"Come on in," Sheriff Taylor said, grimacing a little as he opened the door and motioned Mr. Abernathy in and toward one of the chairs. It was the closest to the large desk, which sat formidably in the center of the room. The chair looked worn upon further inspection, but James said nothing and sat down. The office was sparse but tastefully decorated—various pieces of unmatched furniture, yet all coming together in a not-too-unpleasant fashion.

"As you know, Mr. Abernathy," Sheriff Taylor began speaking, "I'm sure you have been watching the news. This has all come as a big shock of course. Lord knows, Bobby Lee is a real piece of work, but few had realized his true makeup—a natural born killer waiting to be released. It's my personal opinion that he would have killed that little boy had he found him. Now, no telling where he is, but anything's possible." Sheriff Taylor pressed his hands together as he leaned against his desk, the wrinkles becoming very apparent on his forehead. Ayla's dad nodded his head, sitting further back into the chair as Sheriff Taylor continued to speak.

"Once we find Bobby Lee, and yes, I will find him, we will apprehend him and bring this to swift justice. This whole darn community is up in arms right now. All the women are scared, and for the sake of that poor boy that criminal needs to be put behind bars. I just want to make sure that we do everything by the book, nothing that would let this guy find a way to weasel out of the death penalty. I've seen her, you know . . . her body as well as the little boy. It was cold, cruel, and gruesome. This needs to be dealt with so people can get on with their lives. I mean, I can't even get half the ladies in this town to go to the grocery store. Town's like a ghost town. Nobody wants to come out of the house, and I don't blame them. As long as Bobby Lee is not in jail, we are going to have a problem. I called you down here to meet with the child's aunt,

Mrs. Laurie Richards, 'cause I want to get the ball rolling when we do catch him, but I also want to ask you something on a personal level that stays between you and me."

The sheriff moved from behind the desk and sat down in the chair next to Ayla's dad. "Sure," Ayla's dad replied.

"Obviously," the sheriff continued, "Bobby Lee will need to be charged in the death of Christine Putnam, but I'm sure we can get a quick arraignment date and get it moving forward. Judge Leonard, hopefully, will set a bond too high for him to bail out or just deny him bond outright. You know, keep him in jail until trial. Let everybody's nerves calm down and allow things to resume to a somewhat normal pace . . . at least until trial."

"Then it will be a circus," James Abernathy said, watching Sheriff Taylor's eyes for a clue as to what he was thinking. But the weathered sheriff said nothing, only nodded his head. He remembered all too well the circus of media before a big trial, riots, all before Mr. Abernathy's time here in Tate County, but that conversation was for a different time and place. All that would just wind up giving him more bad dreams, and Sheriff Taylor was not willing to think about that right now, so a simple nod would do.

"Now, on to what you wanted to ask me personally?" Ayla's dad pushed a little further up in his chair and closer to the sheriff as he spoke.

"Well . . ." Sheriff Taylor paused. "I was wondering if . . . let's just say . . . someone might want to adopt that little boy, Levi."

Ayla's dad smiled gently. He knew instinctively that the sheriff must have been talking about himself and his wife. Why else would the sheriff ask him to keep it in confidence? "Well, although I do not dabble so much in family law and the children's code, I do know enough to answer your question and hopefully any others you might have. Because of the nature of this incident, you and I both know that child services is gonna get involved and basically do their own little investigation of the situation, which is why I am assuming you want me to talk to the boy's relative and provide her with some legal advice regarding the child placement procedure. Next, they are going to decide who the child's nearest relative is, and then they will have a hearing before the judge to place the child in a suitable home, which is typically that of family member's household."

The sheriff listened intently.

Ayla's dad went on. "If for some unlikely reason the relative would not want to care for him, a person who is not a biological parent or family member could contact the family services office and go through the process of being considered a possible candidate for the child's placement. However, let me warn you, it is a lengthy process and unfortunately is almost always denied. They usually try to either rehabilitate the problematic parent or ship him off to a family member."

Sheriff Taylor's face looked forlorn but pensive. It was evident that he was deep in thought as he mulled over the information about adopting Levi. Ever since he had held that little boy in his arms, he had thought about him. He knew the mother's sister had other children but really didn't have the room nor the finances to take him in. Since he and his wife could not have children, he knew they could provide the love and attention Levi was going to need to get through something like this and develop properly. The problem was being considered. At the moment, some out-of-state relatives had agreed to care for him until a final decision could be made by child services. Although they had expressed no desire to take him in, all parties had felt the child would be safer with them than anyone else while his father, Bobby Lee, was still at large. In fact, the victim's sister and her children were being carefully watched for fear that Bobby Lee might exact some type of vengeance. They had never made any contact with Levi's mother during her tumultuous relationship with Bobby Lee, so it was extremely doubtful he would even be aware of their existence and therefore the best alternative for Levi, given the circumstances.

Still, Sheriff Taylor longed to care for the little boy and everything in his heart told him not to give up, though he had brushed off the idea when he and Lucy had discussed it because he could not bear to tell her if they were denied. However, given this new information, he would speak with Lucy when he got home. If she agreed to try, they would make the necessary phone calls to inquire about adoption.

"Sheriff . . . Sheriff . . . !" Ayla's dad said as he jolted the sheriff from his thoughts. "You okay? I'm not boring you, am I?"

"On the contrary," he said abruptly. "You've actually provided me much insight. Since Mrs. Richards was unable to come by today as I had hoped, I'll give her a call and coordinate a time for us all to meet. Now, let's get you back to your family and me on the heels of a hardened criminal," and with that, he stood up from his chair and shook Mr. Abernathy's hand. "Glad you came to this town; it's important that we have a man like you." The handshake was firm and his gaze sincere.

Ayla's father smiled genuinely again. He liked Sheriff John Taylor and was instantly glad to be of some benefit to him.

As he walked out of the office, he thought of that little boy. Regardless of the sheriff's standing in this town when it came to child services, it was always wise to have legal representation. Perhaps he should have let the sheriff know that he could call him if he needed. Then again, he knew Sheriff Taylor already knew that. The hallway was now awaiting the next shift of deputies to come and relieve the others who had already pulled a double shift.

Because of budget cuts, the county had downsized about eight months ago, and now everyone had more duties and still no raise nor hope of one in the future. But that was neither here nor there. This was a full-blown crisis and everybody was willing to do his or her share and beyond.

The sheriff stood by his chair for a moment as Mr. Abernathy walked out.

He had always been a firm believer in some people having a knack for being able to tell if a person had a good character or not. At church, the preacher had called it discernment. He had agreed but called it "horse sense" because it sounded better.

He knew James Abernathy was good people. Even though he and his family were outsiders to the rest of the townsfolk, Sheriff Taylor and he had hit it off the first time they met. James had struck him as a family man, honest, humble, and genuine. When he had found out that he was going to be the new assistant DA in town, he had laughed incredulously. Just about every lawyer he had come across was more of the swindling type. Sell their momma for a nickel and that kind of thing. But Mr. Abernathy was different. He saw the world as it should be and wanted to make a difference that was positive, which was something he had tried to do since being elected to office, though it wasn't easy, as John and Lucy knew all too well.

Maybe having someone like little Levi would bring happiness to Lucy and rest to him. But most importantly, Sheriff Taylor thought sadly, hope for little Levi. He sat back down in the chair behind his desk, grabbed the telephone, and began to dial. The phone continued to ring until a nasally voice was heard on the other end.

"Hello, Ward County Sheriff's Department, Deputy Fuller speaking. How may I help you?"

Sheriff Taylor let out a groan and bellowed into the receiver. "Deputy Fuller, this here is Sheriff Taylor speaking. Let me talk to Roy. Got us a murder and a murderer loose."

Deputy Fuller pushed a small button on the telephone, which immediately transferred the call to Ward County Sheriff, Roy Faulk. "Roy speaking," the man's voice said quickly. "Sheriff Taylor, is that you? What you doing over there in that county, letting criminals run amuck?" He chuckled at the end of the sentence.

"This is serious, Roy," Sheriff Taylor snapped back unamused.

"Sorry," Roy replied. "Whatcha got? Something I need to have my boys to be on the lookout for?"

Sheriff Taylor grimaced. "Big Roy," as everyone liked to call him, was nothing short of an ego hound, always looking to showcase his boys, which was slang for his deputies on the news or any other media event. He was a rotund man with a receding hairline and hairy arms. He was always calling the sheriffs from other counties when they had caught some drug dealers, made drug busts, etc. At first, Sheriff Taylor would entertain the conversations by replying with oohs and aahs. Nowadays, he just put the phone on his desk and took a nap with his feet propped up as Big Roy continued to rave about his exploits. But now was not the time for egos or ego busting. This was serious and knowing Bobby Lee anything was possible. He knew at some point he would run out of money, or worse, feel caged in and then God help them all.

It wasn't going to be pretty. Bobby Lee was not someone who would just easily give up and turn himself in. He was too much of a rebel and hated the law with a passion.

"Look here, Roy, a fellow by the name of Bobby Lee Putnam killed his wife, Christine Putnam, yesterday at approximately 3:00 p.m. and then fled the scene. Deputy Mark Hunter was the first to arrive at the residence and discover the couple's four- or five-year-old boy, Levi, about scared out of his mind, I would reckon. Anyhow, we took the little boy in, but he's too young to really question. He's staying with some out-of-state relatives right now, but at this point we have no leads as to Bobby Lee's whereabouts. I just faxed over his rap sheet to Deputy Fuller. It's about half a mile long but mostly petty crime. Biggest thing on the rap sheet besides the domestic violence was some forgery charges, disturbing the peace, and a simple burglary, although that didn't stick because someone forgot to read him his rights in Jefferson County so he only saw about a week in jail. It's got his photo and identification as well. Sure would appreciate you being on the lookout for him. He is probably armed, so treat him as dangerous and consider him as such. He's weaseled his way out of the majority of his petty crimes, but he knows this one is serious and he's probably holed up somewhere watching the news about it, so he's bound to be a handful when we do find him."

Ray grunted a few times and then let out a loud yawn. "Sure thing John. I'll see to it my boys are on the lookout, and when we catch him, I'll call you." Roy always had a way of sounding sarcastic, and Sheriff Taylor knew well what Roy meant. Roy would first call the media, then him— he wasn't stupid. This had happened before, in a less serious case, but he couldn't think about that right now. Once they apprehended Bobby Lee, then he could close his eyes and let his mind be flooded by other emotions.

"Okay," he said and let out a loud sigh. At the end of the day, it didn't matter, just as long as they put Bobby Lee behind bars and put to rest everyone's fears.

Roy hung up, and Sheriff Taylor placed more calls and expressed concerns to each and every law enforcement agency throughout the state. He hoped if word got out about Bobby Lee, someone might come forward before it was too late. The news would air the story and his picture on the five o'clock, six o'clock, and ten o'clock news.

With five local channels running the same story and all the police departments and sheriffs' offices being on alert, someone was bound to be called about the incident, and he would be ready. Leaving the office was not an option at this point.

Chapter 10

Hidden

The next call was to Lucy. "Hey, hon," his voice softening as he spoke to her.

"Hi, John. About to cook dinner, you coming home?" Lucy replied.

"No, " he said, pausing for a moment.

Lucy replied with obvious disappointment. "I figured as much, but I thought I might bring you a plate if you're gonna be on duty until you catch him."

"Can't do that now; you'd best stay indoors like everybody else. No tellin' where this guy is and what he's got planned. After the murder, we all know what he's capable of. No . . . it's a nice thought, but stay put."

Lucy could hear the tired and worn tone to Sheriff's Taylor's voice. She was used to it, but knew all too well that he was functioning on less than a full stomach or a good night's sleep. He desperately needed both but probably wouldn't be able to get either one until this Bobby Lee was caught. As they said their good-byes and Lucy hung up the receiver, she pulled her hair up into a chignon and finished stirring the spaghetti. The oven let out a short burst of three consecutive beeps, alerting her that the bread had finished and was ready to come out. So she grabbed the oven mittens and opened the oven door, instantly feeling a gust of warm air against her face as she reached in and grabbed the tray of delicious buttery bread.

She knew he was just worried about everyone, but she was worried about him. The department was only ten minutes from the house. She could make him a plate and be over there and back before her favorite show. Then she would lock the doors and just wait for him to return. She smiled to herself as she thought about her plan. He wouldn't be too upset when he saw what she had made him for dinner. She knew that he needed to eat something if he was going to be up most of the night. It was decided. After eating, she made a plate of the leftovers and grabbed her keys to head out.

The garage was dark, almost eerie, and Lucy suddenly began to wonder if her idea was still a good one. *Be strong*, she told herself, though her stomach was in knots. She took the keyless remote and pressed the button to unlock the car. Funny, it did not beep as usual. *Must have forgotten to lock up when I came home today*, she thought, and opened the door to get in. Everything looked just as she had left it, so she sat down and put the plate of food and her purse on the passenger seat. She noticed her hands were shaking for some reason, so she steadied them and put the keys in the ignition.

The car started with a low purr and then rumbled a bit as the garage door opened. She pressed down on the gas pedal to slowly reverse out of the garage and onto the driveway. The radio was on, but the volume was down, so she turned it up. It was a familiar song, one of her favorites. She began to sing with the music and pat her hands against the steering wheel as she drove as if it were a small drum she beat in step to the music. It helped to calm her as she headed to the sheriff's office.

Normally, the ride seemed so short, but this time it seemed like an eternity. She knew it had to be her nerves, but there was not time for that. Once Bobby Lee was caught, everything would get back to normal and John would be there with her sitting down and relaxing.

She could see the lights of the building as she neared the road but again felt that wave of instant dread and could not shake the feeling that something was terribly wrong. A chill went down her spine, and she tried her best to not appear nervous or worried. She was close enough now to find a parking space, so she leaned forward against the steering wheel and willed herself to focus on her mission. After scanning the area, she noticed an empty parking space not too far from the station. She turned the vehicle into the area, carefully watching the cars that were parked a little closer than they should have been, which created somewhat of a tight squeeze for her vehicle, but still manageable. "Ah," Lucy exhaled, letting out a sigh of relief. She turned off the radio, then the ignition, and slipped the keys into her purse. Opening the door, she steadied her purse and the plate of food as she tried to ease out of the car. Just as she was about to put her feet onto the pavement, she heard a man's deep voice from the seat behind her. "Where do you think you're going, Mrs. Taylor?"

Lucy froze as if transfixed by fear with nowhere to turn. John was right; she should have never left the house. Suddenly, visions of them finding her body directly in front of the sheriff's department flooded her mind. She wanted to let out a scream and yet nothing came from her mouth. She knew that Bobby Lee would not hesitate in killing her if she tried to run. There was no way to bridge the distance from the front door of the station and her vehicle without him catching up to her. She could feel him straightening his body behind her as the cold blade of the knife touched her neck and pressed into her delicate skin, reminding her of his sinister motive.

"I said, where do you think you are going, Miss Priss?" Bobby Lee sneered as he spoke.

Lucy wasn't sure if she should say anything. "I'm . . . I'm going to see my husband," she quietly mumbled, almost feeling like the voice was not her own. It seemed so strange and so small.

"Your husband, huh?" Bobby Lee said, this time pushing the point of the blade a little more, causing her to almost choke. Tears began to fall.

"Yes, yes," she stammered, forcing the words from her mouth. "He's expecting me." It was a white lie, of course, but maybe Bobby Lee would think that he was being watched and walk away, but she was wrong.

"Really," he said and laughed manically. "I hope so. Time to show this town what I'm made of and that two-bit piece of garbage sheriff we got runnin' things."

Lucy could now see his face coming into view as she looked into the rearview mirror. It was devilish and dirty. His eyes were sunken in and sweat beads had formed around his brow. He must have been hiding in various places since the murder, which probably did not afford him a bath or food. She grew more terrified. As he laughed, he lifted his other hand up and, wrapping it around the seat, grabbed at her hair, pulling her neck back as he spoke again. "I'm in luck. Once he sees me with you, he might have to step down from his self-righteous throne in there and listen to what I've got to say."

Letting out a whimper, Lucy closed her eyes and tried to stop the stream of tears that kept running down her cheeks. *Think . . . clear your mind . . .* she thought, but this was easier said than done. Fear gripped her now, and her own body's recognition of true danger was almost overwhelming. "I'm sure . . . he'd listen to you," she stammered. Lucy remembered hearing about a story she had read where an attacker had let his victim go after a lengthy conversation. It was worth a try, anything to stay alive and alert until maybe someone would see her vehicle and say something to somebody . . . anybody.

He pressed the tip of the blade closer to the center of her neck and sneered, "No, I don't think he will; he ain't interested in what I want to really say or what I really think. Him and those other fellows who call themselves the law don't impress me at all. I've been just sittin' back and watching him chase me like a dog chases his dang tail. Yep . . . just watchin' them try to outsmart me."

Lucy knew that wasn't true. The closer he got to her, the more she could smell the repugnant odor of sweat, beer, and dirt. He was filthy and, despite what he said, still had some fear of the law or he would not have run and hid for so long. However, she steadied her voice as she spoke. "Well, I don't know what they've been doing or not been doing. I'm not the law; I'm just married to it. Maybe we both can just call him together. Hmm, what do you say?"

Slapping the back of her head as hard as he could, he laughed as he spoke. "I'm gonna let you do the talking or at least your body."

"What . . . what do you mean?" she said. But she knew. He meant to kill her and use her as the message. It suddenly became very obvious to her that if she didn't do something quickly, there would be no chance of her survival. It was clear that his mind was already made up. All the talk was just his way of toying with her and wasting time.

Her heart began to beat faster. She closed her eyes and took a deep breath. His glassy eyes were transfixed on her, but he could not read her mind, and she was not going to let him just paralyze her with fear. No doubt he had done that to the poor girl. Her fear and her love for this disgrace of a man cost her her life. Determination kept her focused as she quietly moved her hand from her lap to her side.

Earlier when she had prepared to leave the house, she put her cell phone into the small compartment attached to the door and just a few inches from her seat. If only she could just put her fingers on it. The phone had a small button just for emergency calls, never thinking she would ever need that button and, if so, never like this. However, for this to work, she was going to have to keep him talking long enough to distract him. Though it would not take her out of danger, at least someone would know what was happening. The possibility or slightest chance of help was worth it.

"You have a son, don't you?" Lucy said quietly, still trying to slide her hand toward the phone without being noticed. The back of her head still hurt, and she was still a bit stunned from it but remained focused. Bobby Lee was clearly not prepared for her comment. For a second, he almost looked human, and then he grimaced as if in a vicious fight for his sanity.

"Who's got Levi?" he asked angrily.

"I . . . I don't know. I just thought you might want to know that they found him . . . that he is okay." Lucy bit her lip and scanned his face for any signs of emotion as she spoke. Her right hand was now at her side slowly feeling its way in the dark for the phone. Afraid that the slightest move would be detected, she inched her fingers slowly, gently down the seat and into the small compartment. Her long, slender fingers traced the sides until she felt something metal, something square, something familiar. Her phone. Only it had moved a little too far out of her reach from being jostled to and fro as she had been driving. Of course, she hadn't noticed anything because she had turned the radio up. *Oh, no!* It was near impossible to extend her hand far enough without positioning her body forward. Bobby Lee still had the knife pressed against her neck, just pricking the soft skin, reminding her of his control.

"Don't you care if he's okay?" she blurted out, trying to be a little more forceful as she tried to disguise her body movements.

"What's it to ya, you self-righteous whore?" he snapped. Lucy shuddered. Maybe she had gone too far. The idea wasn't to anger him.

"I just thought—"

"You just thought, huh?" Bobby Lee interjected. "What did I tell you women about thinking . . ." he started, this time drawing close enough to whisper in her ear and making her wince. It was hard to not let his words scare her. There was no remorse. It was almost as if a sense of pride crept through the timbre of his voice and resonated in the air. He was heartless and did not deserve to see the light of day.

"I'm telling you what I think, that's all. You don't have to like it . . . you don't have to agree," she said as she straightened a bit more forward, boldly expressing her disdain for him. This time, she allowed her fingers to reach out and grab the end of the phone and slide it a little closer to her, until she finally had it firmly in her grasp. The knife was causing significant discomfort, but something inside her helped her to remain calm.

Meanwhile, Sheriff Taylor was putting a couple of quarters in the dilapidated snack machine. It was not much of a selection, but he was hungry and starting to really get tired. A few phone calls had come in but no real leads on Bobby Lee's whereabouts. The general consensus was that he had up and left town and was probably in Mexico or Canada by now. He had reminded the townsfolk that the curfew was still in effect and would continue until they finally apprehended Bobby Lee. Much to his delight, most people were so afraid to come out thinking that a murderer was still on the loose that he had allowed two of his deputies to return to their families for the night, but they needed to remain on call as needed.

The sheriff pressed the button and a small bag of peanuts teetered its way down and fell to the bottom of the dispenser. He pushed his hand through the small window and grabbed them. Boy, he sure did miss being at home with a nice warm meal and Lucy by his side. He thought about giving her another call but figured she probably just watched the news and retired early to bed. *No sense in waking her.* He looked at the small bag of peanuts and shook his head. *Probably half a decade old,* he mused. *Oh well, this is about as good as it's gonna get,* and he opened the bag. Sitting down on a nearby chair, he stretched his legs out and let out a tired yawn. Lately, he had been so busy that he hadn't had much time to talk to Lucy about possibly adopting Levi. Although he knew what she would say, that wasn't the point. After twenty-six years of marriage, they discussed everything together, without exception. Once Bobby Lee was behind bars and he could go home, he would sit down with her and discuss what had been on his heart since holding the little boy in his arms. Although they could never know the joy of having a child of their own, little Levi would indeed bring a sense of peace and fulfillment that they both had been longing for. Sheriff Taylor continued to mull over those thoughts as he rubbed his brow and stretched his feet out a bit further.

Ever since he had spoken with her earlier, he had felt a nagging feeling that something wasn't right. Like Bobby Lee was still in town, that the worst was yet to come. But perhaps that was just his nerves. As usual, these feelings seemed to go hand in hand with his line of work. There were times he had thought about just quitting the force, but it wasn't an easy choice. The townsfolk had watched him rise through the ranks and trusted him. More importantly, many depended on him. As much as the job itself was stressful, it also gave him opportunities to help those in need that he might not have otherwise been able to help. Pulling his legs back in, he bent his knees and lifted himself up out of the chair.

Maybe a walk outside to clear his head was the answer. He repositioned his belt and began walking down the hallway, still rubbing his eyes and trying his hardest to stay alert. The hallway was long, but the front doors were in sight.

The four remaining deputies were on duty and out patrolling, which left only the dispatcher in the front office. Gladys had been the dispatcher for the Tate County Sheriff's Department since 1979. *Goodness, she has seen a lot,* he thought. She was a skinny woman in her late fifties with salt-and-pepper hair that was always in a large bun on top of her head. She had brown eyes and wore thin spectacles that were attached with a small beaded wire that wrapped around her neck. She let her glasses hang every once in a while when she needed to rub her eyes and take another sip of Diet Coke, which she did often.

He really had never seen Gladys express emotions except that one time . . . and as he thought about it, he closed his eyes and grimaced. The past was always just under the skin—ever present and constantly coming to the surface to wreak havoc again. Gladys had been the only other person it had affected so strongly. As usual, she had taken the call, had been familiar with the little girl, and when he and Deputy Charlie had discovered her body, it had revealed a side to her that no one really believed existed—a typically crass woman, yet softened for a moment by tragedy. Months later, she had still been attending some "grief counseling groups" paid for by the department but for what Sheriff Taylor never asked. Had she known the young girl for a long time or was it just how it had happened? Maybe it was even something in her past that brought up bad memories. No one was ever going to know though because Gladys never said anything more about it. Just went right back to answering calls and sipping on her Diet Coke.

Sheriff Taylor walked out the front door and leaned against one of the columns located at the entrance to the department. Only the lights beaming down from the top of the building gave visibility to the entrance. He yawned as he surveyed the parking lot. Only his vehicle and Gladys' old Buick were parked near the front of the building. Putting his hand to his forehead to see past the glare of the lights overhead, he thought one of the vehicles parked further down looked just like Lucy's. *Man, I must be seeing things*, he thought. *She wouldn't have come out and not walked in.* His heart began to beat faster, knowing full well that he had asked her to stay put. "Darn it, woman," he uttered.

"So, where are you?" Sheriff Taylor said to himself as he fumbled in his pocket and retrieved the small cell phone that she had bought him last Christmas. She had shown him how to save certain telephone numbers into the phone and though he didn't fiddle with it too much, he could make a phone call from it when he needed. After scrolling down to her number, he pressed the button to begin the call. Then pressing the phone to his ear, he heard it ring, then something else—breathing, a shrill scream, then nothing.

Before realizing what had just happened, he instinctively began running toward the vehicle parked in the distance. Something told him that she was there and in danger. As he got closer, his steps felt as if he were running in slow motion. His mind raced, but his feet felt sluggish and heavy.

In the car, Bobby Lee was screaming, but not in fear. Only anger escaped from his voice as he released the knife from the body of Lucy Taylor. When he heard the phone ring, he stabbed her as she went to grab the phone and yell out for help. Her body had leaned forward, which forced him to thrust the knife deep in her side. She wasn't moving, and it made him scream angrily. He had plans for how he wanted Sheriff Taylor to discover her, and now his carefully thought-out plans were no longer an option. Out of the dark, he could hear the footsteps of someone running toward them, knowing it was now a matter of all or nothing. *I didn't have time to finish her off properly,* he thought and jumped out of the back seat of the car, coming face-to-face with the object of his intentions—Sheriff Taylor.

"Well, well, . . . Sheriff," Bobby Lee sneered. His hand still held the bloody knife.

Sheriff Taylor's face turned pale, but his hand was steady on his holster. He could see the bloodstain on the knife, and all he could think about was Lucy. Was that her blood? Was she still alive? "Bobby Lee, put your hands up," he said, unhooking his gun from his holster and lifting it up in Bobby Lee's direction. It was the first time that anyone had really ever given him cause to point it at them. The drills had been practiced repeatedly in his law enforcement training, but in all these years as deputy and then sheriff, no one had really pushed the limits of his authority like Bobby Lee Putnam. He was nervous but worried more than anything for Lucy. If she was hurt, but still alive, then time was of the essence, and he needed to apprehend Bobby Lee and get him under control as quickly as possible.

Bobby Lee inched a bit closer, seemingly in his own little world and completely unafraid of the gun pointed at him or the harsh words of the sheriff as he continued to echo a warning. Closer and closer he continued to inch his way toward the sheriff, laughing to himself as if he thought of something funny that no one knew about.

"I told you to put your hands up, Bobby Lee!" This time, Sheriff Taylor raised his voice, releasing the safety off the gun.

"Why, Sheriff? Think you scare me like everybody else? You ain't nothing behind that stupid badge and I know it."

"Bobby Lee, I'm telling you one last time; put your hands up before this ends up real bad."

"Go ahead, shoot me. I ain't gonna stop. And when I get to you, I'm gonna slice you just like I did Christine and your wife." The sheriff's heart skipped a beat as Bobby Lee finished his sentence. If this was true, there was no hope for this kinda evil and now he knew for sure that the blood on that knife was his wife's.

Bobby Lee inched a few steps closer and suddenly stopped. The sheriff could see his glassy eyes and the smell of body odor and sweat. His hand stayed positioned on the gun, and he refused to take his eyes off of Bobby Lee. He knew this was it, knew that Bobby Lee was not going to back down, knew deep down that he would never be taken alive. A moment of silence rested uneasily between them as Bobby Lee glanced around with the knife in his hand, letting it catch the light as he giggled to himself.

Sheriff Taylor put his fingers on the trigger of the gun and yelled out again. "For the last time, you better put your hands up! You are under arrest for the murder of Christine Putnam, and I am going to see that you pay for it!"

Bobby Lee turned to face him, but this time not with his maniacal laughter. No, this time in defiant anger. He lunged with knife in hand directly for the sheriff and then in a second it was over. A single shot rang out in the moonlight and found its mark as Bobby Lee's lifeless body fell to the ground. Sheriff Taylor breathed a sigh of relief and regret as he rushed to check Bobby Lee's pulse. He was indeed dead and no longer a threat to anyone, including little Levi. He ran to the vehicle and there, slumped in the driver's seat, was Lucy.

Blood had soaked its way across the bottom of her shirt and onto her pants. Sheriff Taylor gasped at the amount of blood and put his hand to her neck to see if he could detect any vitals. A faint heartbeat quickly renewed his spirit, and he dialed 911 for the ambulance, still holding her frail body and trying to resist the urge to emotionally fall apart. "Hey, it's Sheriff Taylor. Send an ambulance to the department as soon as possible. My wife's been stabbed. She's got vitals, but just barely."

He hung the phone up and shoved it into his pocket. Looking at her made him realize she had been there for a while. He tried not to think about it, but he couldn't help it. All this time he was safe inside, never knowing what she was going through. He knew she had come here for him, the plate of food she had cooked still rested on the passenger seat untouched. If she died, he didn't know what he would do. She was his life, his joy, his everything. A lone tear rolled down his face as he prayed for her to hold on.

Chapter 11

Fighting for Life

Seconds later, the whirling noise of the ambulance and lights came to a skidding halt behind the car. Two paramedics jumped out and began removing her from the vehicle, while feverishly working to examine any and all vital signs. Everything appeared to be whirling around to the point of dizziness and yet in no more than a few minutes, she was in the ambulance with an oxygen mask over her face and an IV line already in her left wrist.

When Gladys had heard the commotion of the gunshot, she had called all the deputies back to the department, so the parking lot was set ablaze by whirling lights, although Sheriff Taylor wasn't really paying attention. He gave a few nods here and there, and then he jumped into the ambulance by Lucy's side. She seemed so small and fragile, almost childlike with her thin frame and her long hair cascading over the side of the metal stretcher. Sheriff Taylor glanced at one of the paramedics as he stretched out his hand to cradle hers. The paramedic nodded back sympathy, and the sheriff tightened his grip, afraid to let her go. The ride was almost unbearable. A few miles seemed like hours and by the time they reached the hospital, she had already gone into cardiac arrest. Upon their arrival, Sheriff Taylor jumped out of the back doors far enough away from the paramedics who, once again, were working feverishly as they rolled her into the hospital. A mass of nurses and lab coats ushered her through the sliding glass doors and whisked her quickly down the hallway. Sheriff Taylor chased after them, trying to watch where they were taking her. They turned down a few more hallways, but he caught up to them and touched the tip of her fingers before she disappeared behind large, gray swinging doors.

Sheriff Taylor knew they were about to operate on her and finally broke down as he walked back to a small group of plastic chairs in the hallway. They were bright yellow and looked as if they had been an afterthought. Maybe someone had complained about only being allowed to wait for their loved ones in the small waiting area or lounge as they called it. It was a good distance down the hall and for once, now that it was happening to him, seemed too far away from the wife he loved so much. He was glad they put the chairs there. If any of the doctors appeared, he would be the first to see them, hear their words, and discern the slightest detection of facial expressions, good or bad. He didn't want to think about the bad, but as a law officer he had to look at all things objectively. However, as a husband, he was not about to give up hope. It was hard to fathom in his mind what all had happened within the last two hours. It felt like a dream he woke up from, not reality.

Sheriff Taylor continued to try to maintain his composure even though the minutes turned to hours, and he continued to feel the urge to barge through the doors and demand to know what was happening. After five hours had passed, his eyes began to droop and he dozed off. He was thinking of their wedding, how nervous he had been, and how beautiful she looked that day.

They had been young, looking at their first home, silly moments, previous sentiments, and passionate memories. The dream made him feel warm, comforted, and happy. But it did not stay transfixed, as he suddenly felt sadness. The baby they had always wanted, finding out they couldn't, the stress, his nightmares, and now this . . . her fighting for her life in a lonely, dilapidated hospital.

"Sheriff . . . Sheriff Taylor, you awake?" The sheriff looked up startled. He hadn't realized he had drifted in thought and quietly scolded himself. The voice was from a tall man with squinty brown eyes that seemed a little large for his narrow face. His lab coat had the name Thomas Conrad, MD on his left lapel.

"I'm here, Doc. Is everything okay?"

"Well, I do have some news for you, and I hope you will be pleased but keep it, as with everything else, in perspective. Your wife had to be revived twice while the procedure took place." Sheriff Taylor shuddered, but the doctor continued to speak. "She is now stable, but there was significant blood loss, which required a blood transfusion in order to keep her alive. We were able to make repairs to her internally and sutured her approximately thirty minutes ago. She may require an additional transfusion, but for now her vitals are stable and within the limits given the severe physical damage done to her. Now, we will continue to monitor her for the next seventy-two hours, but she is still unconscious. So the immediate danger looks to be resolved, but there are still a lot of variables. Until she wakes from the shock-induced coma, there is no telling the damage it has done to her mentally, now or in the future."

Sheriff Taylor nodded his head in agreement with the doctor. The news was bittersweet. She would survive, but in what capacity? He knew there was nothing he could do but pray. It was up to God at this point, and he squinted his eyes to hold back the tears. "I'll check back with you in a couple of hours," the doctor said, touching the shoulder of Sheriff Taylor as he left.

"Sure thing, Doc," he said, then he paused and turned to the doctor. "Thank you for helping to save her." The doctor smiled back and walked into the next operating room. The sheriff sat back on the chair again. It was going to be a very long night, but already he felt a very big weight off of his shoulders. He needed to start thinking clearly again and put everything into perspective, just as the doctor had urged. He stood up and walked down the long hallway again and through the lobby. Once outside, he took his cell phone out of his pocket and dialed the department dispatcher who picked up the phone.

"Gladys, it's me, John."

"We were all worried about Lucy. Is she okay?"

The sheriff could feel his fingers still shaking as he spoke into the receiver. "Doc says he thinks she'll put through." He tried to steady his voice but it was difficult.

"That's good news, Sheriff," Gladys said, relieved.

"It's far from over. She is still in a coma, but the worst I think is behind us." He paused. "Guess you better tell everyone the manhunt is over. Sheriff Roy can send his boys on home, and tell everyone else who is not supposed to be on shift to go home. I'm assuming they transported Bobby Lee's body to the morgue already."

"Sure did, Sheriff. Couple of the deputies took pictures before they moved him for the file, but after that, the coroner came out, pronounced him dead, and transported him to the morgue. I'm assuming the coroner is working on his report."

"Okay," the sheriff said, taking it all in. "I'm gonna go back on inside and try to find me somewhere comfortable to sit for a while; looks like it's gonna be a long night," and with that he hung up the phone.

The sliding glass doors opened for him, and he stepped back inside the hospital. As the hours went by, the temperature dropped significantly and Sheriff Taylor shuddered, suddenly feeling cold. He knew he had the choice of returning back to the two chairs but had honestly hoped that Lucy would have been given a private room by now. At least in there, he could keep a close eye over her, hold her hand, and hear her heart beating. With those thoughts, he decided to walk a bit further down the hallway. He recalled passing a nurse's station somewhere, but he had been in too much of a panic when Lucy had been brought in to really remember where it was exactly. After a few dead ends, he passed an area with a small sign indicating the cafeteria, the emergency room, gift shop, pharmacy, and at the very bottom of the list, nurse's station. He was going in the right direction, so he quickened his pace.

A lone nurse sat behind the small desk area. Though there were many chairs around, all the others were empty. *Maybe I'm at the wrong station?* But just as the thought entered his mind, she looked up as if she either read his mind or felt his presence there. She was a petite brunette with large green eyes and a kind smile. Her hair was pulled up in a ponytail, but a few strands had fallen, framing her face.

"Hi," she said cheerfully. "May I help you?"

"Yes, I'm here with my wife, Lucy Taylor. She was just in surgery, and I had stepped out for a moment to make a few phone calls and wanted to be sure I hadn't missed them putting her in a room. Is there any way for you to check?"

"Of course," she said, and quickly stared intently at a small monitor. After a few moments and some quick key strokes, she replied happily, "Here she is; I've found her. Yes, she has been moved to a private room. Looks like room 619. Why, it's right down that way," she said, lifting out of her chair and stretching her hand out to point to her left.

Sheriff Taylor nodded his appreciation and walked down the hallway looking for her room. 603, 604 . . . walking a bit further and only stopping when he reached 619. He closed his eyes, took a deep breath as he muttered something under his breath, and opened the door gently. A dim light glared onto the bed and illuminated the small frame of his wife. A single chair sat a few feet away from the bed with a TV hooked to some sort of wall mount in the far corner. The sheriff noticed the oversized bathroom, obviously to accommodate various needs of patients, and two IVs dripped a clear liquid into her wrist, but other than that, everything else was still. He could see by the monitor that her heartbeat was regular and that she was breathing, a relief to say the least. But the truth was, he did not know what the future had in store for them, especially her. Would she have nightmares too? Sheriff Taylor's eyebrows furrowed. He sat down on the chair and inched it closer to the bed. He took her small hand and put it in his. He brought it up to his lips and kissed her palm. He wasn't sure if she felt him, but it made him feel good to hold her, feel the warmth of her skin, and know that she was out of harm's way.

"I love you, Lucy," he said tenderly, still cupping her hand in his. "I know you might not be able to hear me, but I want you to know that I'm here, that I miss you, and that everything is going to be okay." Lucy's breathing and heartbeat remained unchanged, but that didn't matter to him. She was still alive, still with him and, more importantly, there was still hope. He was not about to give up on her. He breathed a long sigh and closed his eyes, no longer able to stay awake, her hand still in his.

A nurse awoke him during the night as she checked the IVs and made notes on a small chart. He had enough light to look down at his watch and see it was 1:45 a.m. He had been able to get a few hours' sleep, and though it hadn't been very long, it made him feel more refreshed. Her position had remained unchanged, but Sheriff Taylor knew that was to be expected. Everyone knew his wife was a courageous person, but this was going to be her toughest battle by far. His eyes closed slowly again as he repositioned the chair a little closer and laid his head down on the side of her bed.

Morning came too soon, but that was okay. A new day brought new hope, and the sheriff was doing his best to stay positive. Another nurse was in the room checking vitals and writing on Lucy's chart. She looked to be in her mid-forties, somewhat on the heavy side, and a pleasant disposition.

"Sheriff, if you don't mind, I'm gonna have to get around you to check those IVs," she stated firmly, but with kindness.

"Of course, of course," Sheriff Taylor said and hurriedly stood up, pushing the chair back as he did. The nurse smiled back and stepped in front of the IV pole. Noting that they were almost empty, she made another notation on the paper. Then she lifted the hospital sheet to check their placement, revealing Lucy's thin left wrist. The nurse seemed satisfied. She made some additional notes, and pulled the sheet back far enough to reveal the long bandage secured by white tape that stretched across the right side of his wife's abdomen. Sheriff Taylor grimaced, imagining the ugly deep gash underneath. He had come across many gruesome things in his time on the force, but nothing ever prepared you for seeing something like that done to somebody you know, somebody you love. Tears welled up in his eyes again, but he quickly rubbed them away from the corners of his eyes and continued to pay attention to the nurse.

"Well, looks like I'm all done here," she said matter-of-factly. "The doc should be making his rounds by 7:30 so you've got a little while." Sheriff Taylor nodded his understanding and sat back down as the nurse left the room. His stomach was making weird noises, and he could feel a headache starting to form, but none of that really mattered at that very moment. Once he met with the doctor, he could get a better understanding of what to expect.

She was still unconscious and from the looks of it, hadn't moved an inch since he had arrived. He stretched out his hand and rubbed her forehead. He brushed away single strands of her disheveled hair so he could get a better look at her face. Lucy always hated the way her hair would fall in her face, and he knew if she could, she would be brushing it away herself. He repositioned the sheet back around her small frame, tucking it in some places but keeping it fairly open around the left wrist. The doctor had placed the breathing tube near her nostrils, and he could just hear a faint whistle of air going through the small tube. Hopefully, the doctor would have more information of when she would regain consciousness. After sitting down and dozing off, he awoke with a start. The clock was already well past 7:00, and he knew it wouldn't be too much longer. He leaned over her and kissed her lips softly.

"I miss you, Lucy," he whispered and sat back down to wait for Dr. Conrad. On cue, the doctor rapped his knuckles quickly on the room door to announce his presence.

"Hi," he said, "Got any sleep?"

"A little," Sheriff Taylor said, looking at his wife.

The doctor noticed his gesture and replied, "I know this has been tough and we aren't through the woods yet, but the immediate danger is gone and I really believe that she will regain consciousness. See, unlike most people in her situation now, she did not suffer any blunt trauma to the head, and there was no intracerebral bleeding. Basically, her body was just so much in shock and pain that it just simply turned off, for lack of a better phrase. Kinda like a defense mechanism."

"Does that mean that her case is less severe . . . . that she will wake up sooner or something?" Sheriff Taylor interjected.

"Well, not quite like that, but in a way, yes. She did not suffer brain damage as most cases to losing consciousness; it's more like a prolonged blackout, which can only happen under severe stress or shock. From the small cuts around her neck, it is my medical opinion that one, these were definitely not self-inflicted, and two, these marks happened prior to the actual stab wounds entering the side and abdomen and damaging the tissue and organs underneath. So, suffice it to say, her body and mind were under immense strain. One could easily see why her body reacted the way that it did." Dr. Conrad paused between thoughts and spoke again, this time a bit softer and quieter as if he needed to whisper. "She must have been conscious at least until after the actual stab wounds because there was a lot of blood loss. She needed multiple pints when she was brought in." He paused again, looking directly at the sheriff. "Normally, I wouldn't be that graphic, but I know you can handle it, with

113

your work and all." Sheriff Taylor bit his lip. Although the doctor was right, it still didn't help him swallow it down any easier. He wasn't happy about how everything had transpired, but he couldn't go back in time. No one could have anticipated what had transpired.

"Doc, I sure appreciate everything you did for my wife. I owe you a debt of gratitude. I'm just hoping that someone can tell me how long something like this usually lasts. Hours, days, weeks?" He gulped.

"It's hard to say. Each person, and there's not been many, is different. The answer to your question is yes, there is someone who can tell you—your wife. Only she can decide that. Her mind, her senses. My advice is to just sit back and talk to her. I've known people who swore on the Good Book that people can hear sounds, even when comatose. So, just do as I say and pray about it."

Sheriff Taylor looked at Dr. Conrad. "Pray?" he said credulously.

"Yep, pray. Don't think that I made it this far without seeing first hand that somebody was helping me from above." With that, Dr. Conrad patted him on the left shoulder again and walked away.

The sheriff sat back down in the chair and heard a familiar noise—the short shrills of his cell phone. He reached into his right pocket, pulled it out, and viewed the number on the screen. Though he didn't really recall the number, something was familiar about it so he flipped it open and spoke.

"Hello, Sheriff Taylor speaking."

"Sheriff, it's James Abernathy," Ayla's dad yelled back into the receiver.

"James, let me call you right back. I'm in the hospital right now, as I'm sure you've heard, and I'm technically not supposed to be on a cell phone in the hospital. Once I walk outside, I'll call you back."

He stood up, stroking her hand and arm once again. "I'll be right back," he whispered and walked down the winding hall, past the lobby area, and again through the sliding glass doors. He quickly dialed the number back and Ayla's dad picked up the phone.

"James," Sheriff Taylor said. "It's me."

"Yes, I am here, Sheriff. I actually wanted to tell you how sad I was that this happened, but that my family and I are here if you need anything," Ayla's dad said sympathetically.

"Thank you, James. I'll keep that in mind. She's stable right now, but still in a coma. Doc doesn't really know when she might regain consciousness, but he's pretty positive about the outcome. At first, I was beside myself, but I trust this doctor. He's young, yet I see the sincerity in his eyes. I'm gonna have to resume some of my normal duties but don't want to leave her side. Perhaps, one of your girls wouldn't mind sharing some of the shifts with me if that's not imposing too much. That way I can be here the majority of the day, but see to the other pressing matters. What do you say, any volunteers?"

Chapter 12

The Encounter

"Ayla!" her dad called out.

"What is it, Dad?" Ayla could see her father on the telephone in the kitchen, but his hand covered the receiver as he spoke.

"Ayla, I need a big favor from you, if you are open to it?" Ayla looked at her father quizzically.

"Okay, okay."

"You know that Sheriff Taylor's wife was stabbed by that fugitive, Bobby Lee, and is in a coma right now at the Tate County Hospital. The sheriff has got to go to the office sometimes to still run things but is kinda in a pickle because he doesn't want to leave his wife by herself. He asked me if one of my girls would be interested in volunteering for the job, and I instantly thought of you. He's on the phone right now waiting for an answer and I'd like to tell him yes. Of course, I would be lenient of chores given the circumstances and though it might be for a while, I'd be willing to give you . . . at least $10 a day for helping me extend a much-needed favor." Ayla's dad waited for a response as Ayla pretended to think about it for a moment and then chuckled as she wrapped her arms around her father and hugged him.

"Of course," she said. "I'd do it for free, but since you're offering, you got yourself a deal."

Her father smiled back and lifted his hand from the receiver. "Sheriff, my eldest daughter, Ayla, would be happy to do that for you. Just let me know what time you want me to bring her. She has school, of course, until 3:30, but if that's gonna be a problem a couple of missed days from school won't hurt her. She's already on the honor roll and hasn't missed any days so far this year."

"No, no, after 3:30 is fine. Maybe from 3:45 to 8:30? At least for the time being. I'm sure I'll know even more as the day goes on. It's still morning, but I know the office is gonna be calling me before too long and it would make me feel so much better knowing that someone was here to sit with her while I'm away."

"Consider yourself reassured," Ayla's dad said, and then let out a long sigh and paused. "That's not the only thing I called you about, Sheriff," he said almost apologetically.

"What is it, James?" Sheriff Taylor asked, sounding perplexed at his words.

"Remember what we talked about in your office?"

"Yes."

"Well, child services is all over this one just like I told you they'd be. Seems they are already screening all kinds of family members right now and a hearing for little Levi's placement has already been scheduled for some time next week." James paused, letting the words sink in. "I didn't want to have to tell you with everything else that's going on, but it was the right thing to do, so without trying to put more on your plate, I'm just letting you know that if you and your wife still want to fight to adopt that boy, you are gonna have to pick up the pace or a decision will get made before you've even had a chance to get involved."

Sheriff Taylor paused, mumbling something inaudibly under his breath, then replied, "Who do I need to talk to?"

"I've got the number to the child services, but you'll have to ask who the actual case worker assigned to this one is. They should give you that information when you call, but if not, give me a call back and I'll make a few phone calls on your behalf. In the meantime, I'll call the clerk's office and find out just when that hearing is actually set."

Sheriff Taylor took down the number and thanked him as he hung up the phone. James was right; this was the last thing he needed.

But as usual, he had no control over things like that. He still had a lot to be thankful for and wasn't about to let himself become paralyzed by the sheer magnitude of it all. *Stay focused*, he told himself and walked back to the room. He could hear his stomach making more gurgling noises and decided to locate the cafeteria. He needed to put a little something in his stomach and was hoping they would have some nice fresh warm muffins. He could feel himself salivating. He hadn't had anything but the stale peanuts from last night to satisfy his appetite.

A couple of hallways down, he saw the sign again that pointed an arrow in the direction of the cafeteria. Twenty yards down there were two doors labeled cafeteria. He could smell the food while still outside in the hallway and hear the clanking of dirty dishes being whisked away to the kitchen for cleaning. He pushed through the doors and looked around. On one side of the large room were sets or rows of tables for seating and on the other side large metallic buffet servers with steaming foods in a variety of ensembles. In one area, piping hot waffles, pancakes, and doughnuts adorned the countertop. In other places, fresh bacon, sausage, and country ham. It all smelled delicious and not what Sheriff Taylor expected.

The food was abundant, fresh, and smelled delicious. He quickly found the line of people with trays in their hands and followed right along. The people slid their trays to each of the various stations of food and dished up whatever they had a hankering for. Sheriff Taylor chose a muffin, some grits, a few eggs, and a small slice of country ham. It all looked so good, but enough was enough. He took the tray with the plate and large cup of apple juice to the register.

The lady behind it smiled and began pushing a variety of buttons. "That'll be $6.30," she said, looking up.

"Okay," he replied and pulled out an old, worn black wallet out of his right back pocket. He handed her a ten-dollar bill. He put the wallet back as he waited for the change. "Thank you," he said and shoved the change into his front pocket.

Walking to the nearest table, he sat down and began to eat. It wasn't long before he was finished. The walk back to his wife's room wasn't too bad, now that he had found his way in and out of a few places and had gotten his bearings. After glancing in and seeing she still remained in the same position, he backed out of her room quietly and walked down the hallway to the lobby, so that he could make another phone call to the department.

Gladys would be answering the calls as usual and could pass along any info that might be relevant. He also thought about Mr. Abernathy and what he had mentioned earlier about little Levi. He was going to follow up on that as well while he had a few moments. Outside again, he sighed. Morning had now turned to the beginning of another hot and sticky afternoon. As he took his phone out and dialed the department, he could feel the sweat already beginning to bead across his forehead.

"Hello, Sheriff's Department, Gladys speaking."

"Howdy, Gladys."

"Hey, Sheriff, I was wondering when you were going to be calling in," Gladys said, barely pausing to take a breath. "It's been a media frenzy over here since you left with your wife in the ambulance. Why, we've seen at least two to three news reporters about every couple of hours. Don't know what they keep sticking around for though; the excitement is already over. I think they are waiting on an appearance and interview from you."

"I'm sure they are," he said, "but that's not why I called. What else is going on? Is everyone doing his best to keep things moving smoothly, given the circumstances? You recall how it was last time."

"We are doing our best, Sheriff," she quietly spoke. "It ain't easy with cameras everywhere, but we are still patrolling and taking calls. So, don't worry too much."

"Anything of interest, besides all that?"

"No, not really. Couple of domestic abuse calls. One slip and fall and two calls of vandalism. Seems old man Clemmons saw some young boys on his property and when he went to tell 'em something, he noticed his two weed eaters were gone. I sent Jake out to meet with him and make a report. Other than that, not too much. How's Lucy?"

Sheriff Taylor winced as he spoke. "She's in a private room now, but she is still unconscious."

"Oh, I'm so sorry to hear that. We've all been keeping her in our thoughts around here. When we didn't hear from you, we had thought maybe her condition had improved and you were just preoccupied."

"I wish I could say that," Sheriff Taylor replied. "But the answer is no, she is out of the woods, but still in a coma. She's not breathing or eating on her own, and I just keep hoping that I'm gonna walk back in there and she's gonna be awake and smiling at me."

He tried to hold back tears as he spoke, but there was no point. Many, many times he had remained stoic, always keeping focused, but now was not one of those times. His life would never be the same if she did not regain consciousness. "Sheriff . . . Sheriff . . . you there?" Gladys spoke loudly through the receiver.

"Uh . . . yes, Gladys, I'm here. Sorry. What were you saying?"

"Humph. Well, I was asking what you want us to do while you're not here? Should I let Jake take over for the time being or should I just try calling you from time to time?"

Sheriff Taylor cleared his throat. "No need of that. I'm gonna be letting one of Mr. Abernathy's girls come sit with Lucy while I come in from about 4 p.m. to 8 p.m. each day. At least for the time being. There's a part of me that doesn't want to leave her side, and yet I know there isn't much I can get accomplished just sitting here." He paused as if giving the idea some thought.

"Well, I'll let everyone know," Gladys said and hung up the phone.

Sheriff Taylor looked up into the sky and closed his eyes. "Please God," he said aloud, "Please let her be okay." With his eyes still moist, he pulled his wallet from his pocket and lifted a crumpled piece of paper out, studying it for a moment, then dialed the numbers that were scribbled on it. He felt uneasy, but pressed his ear against the phone as it continued to ring.

Finally, he heard it being picked up and a woman's voice answered. "Tate County, Department of Child Services, Yolonda speaking." The voice sounded irritated, but Sheriff Taylor responded quickly.

"Yes, ma'am, this is Sheriff John Taylor. I was hoping to speak to someone about Levi Putnam." The phone was quiet for a moment.

"Well, you'd better wait a minute. His case is being handled by Ms. Roberta Ross. Let me see if I can locate her." She put the phone down before he could reply. He wiped the perspiration off his forehead. The weather was almost unbearable. He wished he was able to make his calls indoors, but hospital policy had the upper hand. Hopefully, he wasn't going to have to wait too long. A few minutes passed and then he heard the phone being picked up again. "Sir, she's not at her desk. You will have to give her a call back later," her voice was curt.

"Is there anyone who might be able to help me while she's away?" Sheriff Taylor asked nicely.

"No," she said matter-of-factly. "You can call back and ask for her," and with that, she hung up the phone.

Sheriff Taylor was astonished by her rudeness and sincere lack of cooperation, but he put the phone away and resolved to not be discouraged in his pursuits. He would try back later today after he had spent some more time with Lucy. He began to walk back to her room, passing the lobby, which was now full of new faces, new ailments. It was about noon, so a few more hours or so and the doctor may be making the rounds again. Perhaps, he had additional news of his wife's condition.

***

Meanwhile, Ayla sat in the school cafeteria. What looked like beef stew and the resemblance of a corn muffin sat atop a green plastic tray in front of her. She could feel her stomach making gurgling noises, but she simply slid the fork around and around in the substance. It did not look appetizing and she suddenly wished she had packed a lunch from home.

Alongside her sat the majority of her classmates, most of which had already gobbled down the food. The rest had been smart enough to bring their own

There were only two more periods after lunch—math with Ms. Cooper and history with Mr. Curtis, both of which she had tests in today. In fact, most of the girls in PE earlier had expressed their distaste for the tests. But Ayla knew it was only because they hadn't studied. Since she had reviewed the notes she'd made before she had gone to bed, she was pretty confident she would be okay. Besides, her dad was taking her later on to sit with Lucy. Ayla continued to stir the contents of her tray, but her mind was elsewhere.

She had been up cleaning the dishes when the news had come on about Bobby Lee. Some of the footage had actually shown him lying on the pavement, but it had not been very close and no pictures had been taken of the sheriff or his wife. The reporter had simply stated that she had been held at knifepoint and that she was transported to Tate County Hospital due to her injuries. The camera had caught various people going in and out of the Sheriff's Department and shown the sheriff's vehicle or maybe it was his wife's. Anyhow, Ayla felt so sorry for her. *I would have been mortified*, Ayla thought, as a chill ran down her spine, causing her to shiver for a moment. How could people be so cruel to one another?

The bell ringing loud overhead caused her to suddenly look up from her daydream. She quickly grabbed her tray and tossed the food into the garbage. She could feel the eyes of one of the cafeteria cooks on her, but she tried her best to not pay any attention to her as she handed her tray through the small slot. She quickly turned around and chased after her other classmates as they exited the cafeteria and headed for their homeroom before the bell rang again. Soon they would have to dash to the next class amongst the other schoolmates in the crowded hallways.

Ayla actually looked forward to her last class period, which was history, her favorite subject. She knew her father would be picking her up and bringing her to the hospital to sit with Lucy, but for now, she had to focus on the assignments for school.

Ms. Cooper's class was next and the test was in Algebra. For some reason, science, English and history had always come easy, but not math. It just left no creativity in Ayla's mind and was therefore boring. But boring or not, Ayla had a test and was going to have to concentrate to bring home a good grade. After that, she could relax for the most part. The history tests were never too hard.

Before long, Ayla was finished with both classes and daydreaming once again while she waited for the final bell for the day. Soon it would ring and everyone would be dismissed, all pouring out at the same time, only to be ushered row by row onto his or her buses or to the parental pickup. Ayla knew, unlike her siblings, she would not be riding the old bus home, nor visiting Mrs. Tilly for a while. From now on, until something changed, she would be picked up from school and doing her homework at the hospital until her father picked her up again.

The bell rang loudly and, for a brief moment, Ayla stepped back to allow some of the other classmates to leave before her. Springing into action immediately after, she adjusted her backpack and darted down the hall. Ayla's father did not like to wait in the long line of parents, so on the rare occasions that he would pick any of them up from school, he would park directly in front of the entrance and wait. Ayla knew exactly where he would be and smiled when she opened the door to find him still sitting in the car waiting for her.

"Hey, Dad," Ayla said cheerfully, opening the passenger door and throwing her book sack onto one of the back seats.

"Hi," Ayla's father replied back, setting down some of the paperwork he had been looking at. Ayla noticed his attaché case resting on the passenger seat. She didn't skip a beat as she lifted it up, sat down, and put the attaché case in her lap. "Still working, eh?" Ayla said.

"Always," he replied and put the car into gear. Ayla quickly pulled her door shut and off they drove.

"Are you still up for watching over Mrs. Taylor?" he asked after he had driven for a little while.

"Of course, I mean . . . why wouldn't I be?" Ayla said, her voice loud and bubbly.

"Just wanted to ask you again now that we are almost there," he said. "I know you will do a good job, Ayla, it's simply that I want to make sure that you are comfortable with sitting in a room watching her. I know the sheriff is needed back at the department, and he would sure appreciate the help."

"I know, Dad. You told me all of this already last night when he spoke with you. I'm totally cool with it. She was nice and I like helping people, so problem solved. Oh, and that ten bucks each day is also gonna come in handy, cuz it's almost summer," Ayla said as she took a quick breath and adjusted her seat belt. Ayla's father smiled and parked the car near the entrance of the hospital. Both he and Ayla stepped out of the vehicle almost simultaneously, and Ayla laughed playfully as she shut the door first.

"Ha, I beat you," she said victoriously and walked around the car to nudge him in his shoulder. He glanced down at her and smiled as they walked into the lobby door. Ayla noticed a few people sitting near one side of the entrance as she and her father made way for an elderly woman being wheeled out. Over all, it appeared mostly quiet, which gave Ayla enough time to look about and take note of her surroundings. The hospital looked like it had recently been remodeled, or at least certain areas of it. Having moved from the city, Ayla was used to larger and newer. Everything and everyone going just a little bit faster pace. But somehow, since being here, she had found comfort in a slower, steadier way of living. Meeting Mrs. Tilly had been a salvation in a way. It provided a nice reprieve from homework, housework, and tending to her younger siblings.

"Dad, think we should ask someone where she is staying?"

"Actually, Sheriff Taylor already gave me the room number. I think all we have to do is locate the number and he will be waiting to greet us. You have never met him, but he's a likeable fellow. Not exactly what you envision from a small-town sheriff," Ayla's dad said as he ushered them through the network of hallways. Before long, she felt her father quicken his pace and spied a tall man standing half in and half out of one of the rooms. Ayla knew it must be the sheriff. She noted his uniform and quickened her pace as well.

"Sheriff," Ayla's dad said somewhat out of breath, "we are here just as I promised, and this is my daughter, Ayla."

The sheriff looked down, his face obviously distraught. "Dear Lord," he said, his voice shaky, his hands trembling.

Chapter 13

The Explanation

Ayla looked up at him, not quite sure how to take his greeting. Ayla's father also seemed perplexed and stared at Sheriff Taylor. The silence seemed like an eternity.

"Sheriff, I don't understand . . . what's wrong?"

"Her . . . she looks just like her . . ." he said, not really making any sense, his face still pale.

"Her, who?" James snapped back defensively.

"You don't know?"

"Know, what, know who? Sheriff, you aren't making any sense. Who does my daughter remind you of?"

"Come in the room," Sheriff Taylor said, "I'll explain further."

Ayla and her father stepped inside, visibly confused but instantly saddened once inside as they came face-to-face with the fragile and listless body of the sheriff's wife. Both she and her father sat down in the chairs situated in the far corner of the room. Ayla continued to hold her father's hand, unsure of how and why she suddenly felt sad and nervous. The sheriff pulled a chair from the other side of the bed nearer to them and spoke as he sat down. "Look, James," he said, "I know this is gonna sound very odd, but your daughter looks just like a young girl who passed away some time ago. I mean," he said, pausing, "they could have been twins. The resemblance is so unsettling. Must've been before you and your family moved here because you would have known had you been here." The sheriff cleared his throat. "I find it hard to believe that nobody has ever said anything to you."

"Well, I have noticed people around here kinda looking at me odd, but I didn't know why. What did you mean when you said 'passed away'? Do you mean she's dead?" Ayla asked incredulously, suddenly recalling her prior conversation with Mrs. Tilly.

"Yes," Sheriff Taylor replied. "That's exactly what I'm saying." He closed his eyes and put his hand to his head as he retold the entire case, his voice faltering at times, but finally finishing.

Ayla and her father sat back, hanging on every word and remaining silent for a few moments after he had finished. "All I know is that I have continued to wake up almost every night since it happened, and I don't know why. I guess I wish I could have done more. I don't want that for that little boy. Once child services has their way with him, there is no telling where he will end up . . ." his voice barely audible as he finished speaking.

Ayla looked at her father, studying his face. She wanted to tell him about her dream and her talk with Mrs. Tilly but wasn't quite sure if she should. Maybe it had been completely unrelated, but Ayla's heart told her otherwise. She now knew the girl in her dream had to be Meg, but what puzzled her was how to tell them without sounding crazy, or at the very least, laughable. This was serious. That little boy's life was at risk. He deserved to belong to people who wanted him and would give, or at least try to give, him the life he deserved. Although Ayla had never met Sheriff Taylor until now, she had heard her father speak of him and knew that her father respected him.

She pressed her fingers together and bit her lip. About to speak, she was interrupted by her father. "Sounds like to me that was just another horrific sad casualty of our system," he said, disgusted with that realization. Ayla's father sat back in his chair and combed his fingers through his hair, still very much in thought. Ayla saw this as her opportunity and spoke.

"Sheriff Taylor, Dad, I have to tell you something." Both men stared at her waiting for her to speak. Ayla again had misgivings whether or not she should tell them, still wrestling with the idea that they would not understand what she now did. At first, the dream had seemed frightening to her, but now she realized it had been a message.

"You said you were having nightmares, Sheriff Taylor?"

"Yes," he said. "Why?"

"Because, I think she is trying to tell you something. You see, this girl . . . this girl who looks like me, well, I've seen her. But not like you may think." Ayla looked directly at them. "Let me start from the beginning. Since we moved here, there have been a few instances in which I have felt downright stared at. I could never place it, no one actually said anything, and when I would mention it to my parents, they just kinda shrugged it off. As sad as I am for that poor girl, at least after hearing your story, this is all starting to make a little more sense to me.

"A few days ago, I was just doing my usual stuff, cleaning up, studying for a test, doing homework, that kinda thing. Well, anyway, I went on to bed and after falling asleep, I had this really weird dream. I dreamt this girl was showing me around an old dilapidated home. I recall that there was a field, and somehow or another, I couldn't help but want to follow her around. After a while, I didn't feel scared anymore, that is, until I saw her in the field reaching out her hands to me, 'cept there weren't any fingers. She said a few words to me and then I woke up. I didn't know what to make of any of it then so I just shrugged it off and didn't tell anyone, that is until now. I think after listening to what you said earlier that this dream is important, and I also think that this girl doesn't want the same kind of thing happening to anyone else."

She looked at them for a response but both of them just continued to stare at her in disbelief. Finally, Ayla's dad spoke. "Ayla, although I think that your dream has some bearing, I am a bit skeptical. It's not to say I don't believe you. It's just that we need to stand up before another injustice is done, regardless of people looking alike or strange dreams. However, in the meantime, we are going to need to make some phone calls to inquire as to the status of the situation."

Sheriff Taylor chimed in. "Already tried, Mr. Abernathy. Didn't get too far." He recalled the story for Ayla and her father.

"That sounds about right," Ayla's father said. "But maybe you and I just need to take this up a notch. Ayla can stay with Lucy and you and I can go visit the local office."

Sheriff Taylor smiled and nodded his head. A look of relief passed across his face. "Sounds good," he said and stood up from his chair.

Ayla and her father also stood up and Ayla bade farewell to her father as Sheriff Taylor bent over the hospital bed and kissed his wife good-bye.

"I love you, honey," he whispered in her ear and turned on his heel walking out with Mr. Abernathy, leaving Ayla alone with Lucy. Ayla positioned her chair closer to the bed so that she could watch her more intently, setting her book sack in one of the other chairs so that it would be out of the way. Although she had a little bit of homework to do, she really didn't feel like pulling the paperwork out just yet. Her mind was too busy swarming with thoughts of Meg. She shuddered. She had been only fourteen years old, Sheriff Taylor had said earlier. Same age as her. Ayla suddenly felt a deep loss for her and was angered by the senselessness of her death. *How could someone take a life in such a fashion and for what reason? Simple hatred? Jealousy?* Ayla knew she didn't have all the answers, but knew she was willing to stand up for justice, even if it cost. She would do her part to help the sheriff, and she knew her father would as well.

Ayla straightened the skirt she was wearing and pulled her hair up into a ponytail away from her face. Lucy lay motionless but Ayla continued to watch over her. Finally, after an hour had passed, she turned the small television set on, lowered the volume, and changed the channels until she found one she liked. It was the History Channel. A familiar show was on and Ayla sat transfixed to the screen, only moving her head to check on Lucy when a commercial would appear. Once while she was watching, a nurse had knocked on the door, and after opening the door, had checked the monitor and Lucy's wrist.

Feeling bored now that her show was off, she decided to go ahead and pull her homework out. She had to write two small essays. One was to be written about economic growth or decline and the other was on the book *Pride and Prejudice*. Although it wasn't an instant favorite, it was tastefully written and Ayla could not help but enjoy the book. The essays were due the following Monday, but Ayla wanted to go ahead and write at least one of the essays by the end of the day. Ayla tugged the pencil out of its place in her book sack and with notebook in hand, began to write.

ECONOMIC DECLINE BY AYLA ABERNATHY.

She continued writing her essay on the decline of the United States' economy, but stood up to stretch her legs, feeling them going numb from being in the same position for so long.

With her back turned, she stretched her arms above her head, took a deep breath, let it out slowly, and sat back down in the chair. Her stomach rumbled, reminding her about the meal she had chosen to forego at school.

Although she did not regret not eating the "mystery stew," she did regret forgetting to ask her dad to take her somewhere to grab a bite to eat before heading to the hospital.

Since it was 6:30 and only a couple of hours to go before he would be returning to pick her up, she could wait, of course; she just needed to bring a snack next time for sure. A quick examination of her pockets revealed thirty-five cents. *Not enough for a snack today*, she thought and slipped the change back in her pocket. *Might as well finish*, she thought, and picked her notebook back up. A few choice excerpts quoted from the material she had gathered to support her essay lay scattered about on her lap, and she quickly jotted down all that she thought might be useful. Before long, she had completed the essay and read through it a couple of times for grammatical errors and such.

Finished, she put the notebook back in her book sack and turned the channels again until she saw another familiar show. She propped her legs up on the other chair and watched it. The time was now 7:34 p.m. Ayla knew her father should be headed there now to pick her up. She was relieved and continued to watch TV. Before the end of the show, Ayla saw her father's face peering in through a small crack in the doorway.

"Dad," Ayla called out, gathering her book sack and throwing it across her shoulder. "I'm so glad you are back, I'm starved."

"Well, your mom cooked some of her pepper steak if you want some of that. Can't say for sure if there is any leftovers by the time we make it home, knowing your brothers, but I could probably call her and ask her to make you a plate now." Ayla's father smiled, waiting for a response.

Ayla shrugged her shoulders. Despite being hungry, she really wasn't in the mood for pepper steak. "Actually, Dad, I kinda wanted a small cheeseburger, if it's not too much trouble."

He looked at her for a moment then chuckled. "Sure," he said, "we just need to wait on Sheriff Taylor. He had mentioned earlier that he would be back here around 8:15. So . . . not too much longer." Ayla's father quickly sat down, but continued to speak. "Anything?" he asked credulously, looking over at Lucy.

"No, Dad, nothing," Ayla put her head down as if disappointed. "It's so sad; it almost makes me want to look away."

"You should look at the positive, Ayla," her father replied. "Things could have been so much worse than what they are." He paused, putting his hands on Ayla's shoulders. "It's hard, I know, to think about why things like this happen to people who don't deserve it, but unfortunately life is never fair. What we must do is look at what is positive, even in the face of negativity. She is here, she is alive, she is getting better, and Bobby Lee is no longer able to terrorize the people in this town or any other."

Ayla stared at him and managed a smile. She knew deep down that he was right. Just like the girl in her dreams, she must not dwell on such things, but instead find ways to not let it happen again. "Dad, did you and Sheriff Taylor see about that boy that he wants to adopt?"

Ayla's father cleared his throat. "Sort of, but getting information from those people is like pulling teeth," he said, clearly disgusted.

"Did he get him?"

"Well, not exactly, Ayla," her father replied, letting out a long yawn. "He is going to have to attend a hearing, and I will have to file some necessary paperwork in order to even discuss the darn thing with them. I've about had—"

A sudden knock on the door caused Ayla's father to stop speaking. Sheriff Taylor pushed the door far enough to walk inside and closed it softly behind him. His face looked a little more worn since Ayla had seen him last. "Evening, Ayla," he said. "Any good news?"

Ayla looked up at him and back at her father. "No, sir," she replied sadly.

Sheriff nodded his head looking forlorn. "Well, you both are ready to head out, huh? I'd like you to know how much I appreciate you taking the time to support me and my wife. I just . . ." he paused, wiping away the tears, "just cannot thank you enough." Ayla's father put his head down trying to hold back his own emotions.

Ayla smiled and extended her hand out. "You know, I will do what I can, Sheriff."

"Yes, now it's time to go on to your family," he said.

Ayla and her father left the room and walked down the lighted hallways until they reached the lobby doors and outside. The air was thick and muggy, nothing like where they had moved from. Large mosquitoes flew close by and Ayla could already feel the sweat beads starting to appear on the back of her neck. Once inside the car, the mood, although sober, seemed a little more relaxed. After starting the car, Ayla's father spoke briefly about the day's work until they reached the hamburger joint in town. It was a typical fast-food restaurant. Ayla's heart was set on a cheeseburger now that her time with Mrs. Taylor was over. "Dad, I'd like a junior cheeseburger," Ayla piped up as her father drove up to the drive-through.

"Do you want fries and a drink?" he asked.

"Nope, just the cheeseburger."

Ayla's father ordered the food. Soon after, the lady returned to the window and handed Ayla's father a small bag. He passed it on to her as he rolled his window back up and headed for home. Once there, Ayla grabbed the remainder of her leftover cheeseburger and her book sack out of the car. It had been a long day, and she was glad to finally be back home. Much to her amazement, the kitchen was clean and only a few items here and there littered the living room floor. She smiled, glad to not have too much to do now that she was finished watching the sheriff's wife.

Heading to her room, she thought about Mrs. Tilly. It would be a while before she would be able to visit and discuss with her the latest news, a thought that disappointed her. Nevertheless, it was an unavoidable situation, now that she would be at the hospital every afternoon. Sitting down on her bed, she closed her eyes. There was still some more homework, but she did not feel like doing it. Nothing but a warm bath would suffice. Pulling her pajamas out of one of the chest of drawers, she walked to the bathroom and turned the faucet on.

***

Meanwhile, the sheriff sat quietly in the hospital room. The nurse had assured him that the doctor would be making his rounds in the morning, and he would be able to ask whatever questions he may have. Although initially he had been optimistic, seeing her unable to gain consciousness left nothing but remorse and a lump in his throat. Her hands had remained as motionless as when he had first sat beside her in her room, holding them in his and praying that she would simply wake up. Nothing seemed further from that now. Food continued, like clockwork, to be brought into the room, only to get cold and then later removed.

He wondered how long it would take for recovery or if there would ever be one. He shuddered just thinking about those who, left in his position, had the impossibly painful choice of whether or not to allow them to stay in a vegetative state or "pull the plug." Shaking his head as if to clear the very thoughts out of it, he stood back up again and rubbed his eyes. The chair offered very little comfort, but he would have to make it work another night, much to his regret. "Darling," he said, looking at his wife. "I wish things could just go back to the way they were." Deafening silence followed. He pulled the chair back to the side of the bed, put his hand over his wife's hand, put his head down, and fell asleep.

***

The bath was refreshing and Ayla stepped out of it feeling energized. Though it had gotten dark, this was just what she needed to help her finish up her homework. The final essay was about a book she had already read and enjoyed. Pulling the book out, she copied the title and author's name on a blank page in her notebook. After only thirty minutes, she reread what she had written and smiled with satisfaction.

She put it back into her folder and shoved the folder and notebook in the book sack. A knock on her door startled her. "Yes, what is it?"

Her dad entered the room. "I thought you'd like to know," Ayla's dad said, staring intently at her.

"What, what's wrong?"

"Nothing, honey," Ayla's dad said, taking a seat at the foot of her bed. "Sheriff Taylor's wife just opened her eyes. He's calling *everyone*."

Chapter 14

_____

A Miracle

Sheriff Taylor beamed from ear to ear. "I had just dozed off," he said sleepily, telling the nurses, "when I felt something brush over my hand. I kinda twitched my fingers a little and looked up. I thought I was dreaming when I saw her eyes open just looking at me. I tell you I 'bout jumped out of my chair, praising God." The nurses nodded as if listening while they checked Lucy's breathing, heart rate, and pupils.

"I've already put in a call to Dr. Conrad; his nurse said he would be arriving shortly," one of the ladies said to the other.

Sheriff Taylor continued to stand away from the bed as the nurses worked around one another. He had called just about everyone to share the news. Her parents, filled with joy and heartfelt gratitude, were already on the road headed there.

"Honey," Sheriff Taylor said happily, "your parents are still on their way to come and see you. I hope you aren't feeling overwhelmed, but everyone is just so happy that you are going to be okay. You had quite a few people praying for ya." Lucy smiled at him, though her head still ached and her memory of the last week seemed vague. It frustrated her, but she did not want to dwell on that. Waking up to see her husband's face, being alive . . . that's all that mattered at this moment.

Once the nurses had left, the sheriff could still hear their voices in the hallway. He smiled. Many of them called it a miracle, and he could only agree. He was anxious to see the doctor and hopefully discuss when she would be able to return home.

"I . . . I am just confused right now, John," said Lucy, replying to his earlier response.

"Oh, I know, well . . . I'm sure you must be," he said, rushing to her side.

"What happened?" she stammered. "The last thing I recall is Bobby Lee Putnam. I . . . was in the car and he was threatening you. I . . . can't remember much after that," she said sadly. "I just remember being so scared."

Sheriff Taylor cupped his hands around her face and felt her tears fall. It made him want to cry as well, cry for her. But he closed his eyes and let out a small sigh. "It's okay now, honey. I'm sure the doc is gonna tell us how long it's gonna be before your memory gets better. Fact is, you shouldn't even be thinking of stuff like that right now. You are here and safe. I don't know what I would have done if you hadn't been all right." He paused, then spoke again. "I've got plenty of things to tell you about, but . . . all of that can wait. Are you hungry?"

Lucy's face grimaced and then her eyebrows furrowed. "I guess I am, just still feel very stiff and my side hurts. What is there to eat?" Sheriff Taylor glanced over at the food tray that had not been picked up yet. It did not look inviting in the least. Walking over to it, he lifted the lid off the main dish, exposing what appeared to be meatloaf. Had it still been warm, it might have done the trick. But after touching his finger softly on the side of the meat, he pulled it back in disgust.

"Well, honey," he said, looking back at his wife, "I'd offer you some meatloaf, but it's as cold as a brick."

"That's okay," she said, yawning softly, her voice still sounding very frail and tired.

"Okay, maybe you should just relax and get some sleep," he replied.

"Sleep?" she said, "I think that's what I've been doing for a while, I'm guessing. How about we just sit and hold one another?" She lifted her hand up slightly and extended it in his direction. It was painful for her, but she knew she had to try. "Please?" she said this time, grimacing with pain.

"Yes, of course," he replied, extending his hand back toward her.

He sat back down in the chair and smiled back at her. Though tired and fragile, she was still so beautiful to him. "I love you so much," he said tenderly.

Lucy glanced back at him and tried to form the words she so desperately wanted to say to him. "I . . . love . . . you, too." Shortly, a short rap on the door broke the moment of togetherness.

"Sounds like I missed all the excitement," Dr. Conrad said, walking in with a big grin on his face. His tousled hair made him look even younger, and he quickly brushed it out of his face as he continued to walk toward them.

"Doc, it's a miracle," John said, echoing the comments of the nurses he had heard earlier.

"Sounds like," Dr. Conrad replied gregariously. He looked at Lucy and extended his hand to her. She slowly pulled her other hand up and touched his with her fingertips. It was too difficult for her, and she quickly let it fall back by her side.

"I'm . . . I'm so sorry, Doctor. There are parts of me that feel okay and others that seem as if they don't want to work, I don't understand." The frustration was apparent in her voice.

"It is perfectly normal after regaining consciousness, Mrs. Taylor. Please don't let these minor things deter you from the goal of having a full recovery. If you haven't been made aware of it yet, you suffered some very serious and life-threatening injuries. You were brought here and have been unconscious until this evening. Your husband has been very worried about you since you arrived, and I'm quite sure he is very relieved to see you awake and even more so because it appears that you are cognitive of your senses and fully aware of your surroundings. Not all cases are like this."

"But I still have no recollection of some of the events that led me here. Will I get my . . . my memory back?"

"I would think so, considering your amazing recovery already." He paused. "Although I would like for you to continue to follow up in my office once you are well enough to return home. And from the looks of it, I would also suggest some very intensive physical therapy for you so that we can rule out any paralysis or nerve damage." Lucy's face looked worried, but she didn't say a word. Sheriff Taylor squeezed her hand trying to comfort her as best he could.

They both knew it would be difficult and that recovery was never easy and most often painful. Each day would have to be taken in stride.

"I think we understand, Doc," Sheriff Taylor chimed in after an uncomfortable pause. Taking the cue, Dr. Conrad made a few more exchanged pleasantries to them both and said good-bye.

That night, Sheriff Taylor slept well, though still in the chair beside his wife. The mere fact that she was back with him in both body and mind renewed his spirits. He wondered if he should tell her about little Levi yet or if he should wait awhile to see how her recovery would be and how quickly she would be coming home. With the recent news of the hearing being so soon, it had kind of thrown him into a whirlwind, and he was not sure how he was going to be able to manage it and Lucy's recovery.

The next day, however, brought clarification to the things that troubled him. Once the nurses had checked on his wife and brought her some breakfast, he walked outside and made a phone call. "James, it's me again."

"Well, good morning, Sheriff. How's Mrs. Taylor?"

"Oh, doing good. I apologize for calling you so late last night to tell you the news about her, but I just couldn't help myself."

"Quit apologizing, Sheriff, nothing was wrong with that. Ayla was very happy for you both as well."

"Tell her again how much I appreciated her looking out for my wife, even if it was only for a day."

Ayla's father chuckled into the receiver. "I will," he replied, still smiling. He drew in his breath. "Is she able to speak? Does she know who you are?"

"Oh, even better than that," the sheriff said happily. "She's aching to be home, though there are some things she doesn't remember. Doc says she's gonna need some PT too."

"Well, I'm sure glad to hear such amazing news. Is she alert enough to discuss Levi?" James asked quietly.

"I don't know, I haven't decided whether or not it would be too stressful on her now or not." Sheriff Taylor paused. "I mean, I want to tell her, but I don't know if she can fully grasp what we would need to do, what the hearing will be about, and whether she can be released in enough time to attend with us."

"You may have to wait a couple of days for her to reacquaint herself with everything and perhaps fill in the gaps of her memory before getting into such a complicated issue. But I will tell you that I would prefer her there if at all possible. I want to be able to show the judge that both of you will be raising this little boy and the kind of environment he will be in with both of you," James said firmly.

"Yes, you're right. Let's just wait awhile and then maybe I can get some feedback from her once she gets a little better."

"That's the idea. Just don't forget we need to go by the child services department and meet this case worker face-to-face, complete whatever requirements they have, and then get ready for the hearing."

"Think your daughter would mind coming over a couple more times so we could get that accomplished?"

"I don't see why not," James replied, and after a few more words hung up the phone.

The sheriff walked back through the doors of the lobby, retracing his steps down the hall to his wife's room. His mind was made up. He would wait a few days to discuss the new developments. Recovery for her was going to be a slow and grueling process, and he did not want any setbacks. Pushing the door open, he smiled as he watched the nurses bring Lucy's breakfast to her. The tray was placed on the small side table and then rolled toward her bed so that she could eat. It pained him to see her face contort with frustration when her hands would not move high enough to lift up the silverware. After a few attempts, however, she had put her fingers around the fork and gripped it enough to push it downward toward the small portion of scrambled eggs. She picked some up and tried to bring it to her mouth. It proved to be a harder task than she realized, and the eggs fell on her hospital gown, mere inches from her mouth.

"Oh, John," she said, looking at him sadly, "would you mind helping me?" Sheriff Taylor nodded. First, he grabbed the food that had fallen and quickly disposed of it. Next, he gently took the fork from her trembling hands and lifted another mouthful of eggs from the tray.

"No reason to look so down and out," he said, thrusting the food into her open mouth. "Doc said it's gonna be tough for a little while and then everything will get better." She swallowed the food and expressed her understanding with her eyes. Though it was painful to see his wife so helpless, before long she had finished most of the food and all of the juice. Color filled her cheeks, and it brought a sense of satisfaction to him.

"Why are you smiling?" she asked, looking at him suspiciously.

"I guess, because you are here, honey. I meant here with me. I know you feel so frustrated not being able to do everything, but you will soon and until that happens, I'm here to take care of you. Good times and bad, remember?"

"Yes, I remember," she said softly. "It's just this feeling like I'm being a burden because I know you've got stuff to do besides being here feeding me eggs." She made a small frown and bit her lip.

"Well, for one, you are not a burden, so best erase that from your thinking, and secondly, it's true I do have to do some things at the office and stuff, but I've made arrangements so that for the few hours that I'm away from you, you won't be alone."

"Arrangements?" she asked.

"Yes, do you remember the new lawyer James Abernathy and his family that recently moved to town, maybe about a year or two ago?"

"Yes, I recall you speaking of Mr. Abernathy, but I've never been introduced. Why would he be watching me while you are away?"

"No, honey, not him, one of his daughters. She stayed with you a little while before you regained consciousness. It was no more than a couple of hours or so, but it did allow me to take care of work that needed tending to. I don't mean to upset you."

She shrugged her shoulders. "I'm not upset, honey. I married you knowing the kind of responsibilities you have. I can't be selfish, even now. I just didn't know what you meant, and I sure don't want someone just sitting with me when I'm well enough to do that by myself."

"I know you can, Lucy. It's as much for my sake as it is yours."

She made another face but stretched out her hand a bit, motioning him to hold it.

Obliging, he spoke again. "I might as well tell you though, you are in for a bit of a surprise. She looks so much like Meg that I almost fainted. Me, mind you, a grown man. It was like seeing a ghost." He paused. "Once I had regained my composure, I explained to them the reason for my behavior. Seems they arrived here a little after it happened and though some of the people in town have given her looks, nobody has ever said anything to her or her father about it."

"Poor thing," Lucy said quietly. "And you, how have you been sleeping?"

"Oddly enough, since all of this has happened, I've actually been sleeping okay. No nightmares. Can't say that they won't happen again, but I guess my mind has been so focused on you and wanting you to be okay."

"Well," Lucy said, thinking for a moment, "guess it would be okay, though I really don't need it. But . . . if it makes you feel better knowing that I've got someone to talk to, then I will comply."

"I think it will do you good," he said happily and put both of his hands around hers as they continued to talk.

***

James Abernathy furrowed his eyebrows as he scanned the documents about Levi. After he forwarded his Motion to Enroll, the clerk had been nice enough to forward him what records had been filed since the case was opened. Though it wasn't too voluminous, there were a few documents that sparked his interest, including the Notice of Hearing. It was another reminder of the urgency, especially if Sheriff Taylor and his wife stood a chance of adopting the little boy. Though this wasn't something he handled on a daily basis, he intended to keep his promise to the sheriff and that meant doing his homework on the new laws regarding adoption proceedings and dusting off those old law books that dealt with this. The paperwork he received would allow him to get up to speed and alert child services of his appearance on behalf of Sheriff John Taylor and his wife, Lucy.

Gathering the pertinent documents, he placed them in a folder along with a checklist of things to be accomplished before the hearing.

Hopefully, Mrs. Taylor can make it there, he thought. He knew that both would have to be available so that he could question them on the stand and so that child services could finish whatever paperwork was required to actually place Levi. Checking the clock in his office, he finished his review of all the documents and, making a few notes, he headed out the door to pick up Ayla from school. It wasn't long before he and Ayla were already back at the hospital and walking toward Lucy's room.

"Gonna be a bit different this time," Ayla's father said as they both continued to walk down the long, illuminated hallway.

"What do you mean?" Ayla asked, readjusting her heavy backpack as usual.

"Well, I mean, she's awake now, so I don't need to remind you to be on your best behavior."

"Oh, yeah," Ayla said laughingly. She knew her father was joking with her. "You don't have to remind me." She gently poked his side.

After a few more steps, they stood right outside the hospital room. "Hope you don't give Mrs. Taylor a scare like you did the sheriff," Ayla's father said quietly, nudging her.

"Gee, I hope not," Ayla replied, pushing open the door as she spoke. No sooner had she said those words than she came face-to-face with Mrs. Lucy Taylor. She was very pretty in a delicate kind of way, and Ayla smiled at her, hoping that she would leave a good impression.

Lucy said nothing, just continued to watch her put her backpack down. Ayla motioned for her father to say something to break the uncomfortable silence.

"Mrs. Taylor, I don't recall having had the pleasure of meeting you, though I've known your husband for quite some time now." He drew a little closer to Ayla. "This is my daughter, Ayla. She will be coming to sit with you for the next couple of days. That is, if it's okay with you?"

Turning her head to give him her full attention, she replied softly, "I suppose my husband feels that it will be beneficial to me to have the company, so in response to you, yes . . . yes, it would be okay with me." Ayla gulped, assuming that Mrs. Taylor was still going to be somewhat disoriented. Perhaps she could still bring some comfort to her, or at least she hoped so.

"Hello, Mrs. Taylor," Ayla blurted.

"Hello, Ayla."

"Well, I guess that's my cue to leave you ladies alone," Ayla's father said, backing up toward the door. "Ayla, I'll be back around eight, just like before," and with that, he was gone. Ayla adjusted her shirt, feeling slightly uncomfortable. It was easy to look over someone who, for lack of a better word, was basically sleeping. She had been able to have uninterrupted time to finish her essays and watch a couple of shows. This was different.

Lucy detected her discomfort and exclaimed, "I promise not to bite, hon! It's okay to come sit by me and talk. My goodness, you do favor that poor little girl. My husband told me that you favored her before he left to go to work, but I didn't realize just how much. She was such a sweet, sweet girl. Wouldn't have hurt a fly. In fact, sometimes I'd see her before I did volunteer work from time to time. Such a shame."

Chapter 15

_____

Hope

Ayla could see Lucy's eyes beginning to water, so she grabbed a tissue from the square tissue holder on the corner table and handed it to her. "Thank you," Lucy said, looking up at her and trying to smile though her eyes continued to tear up at the thought of the young girl who had passed away. "I can see why my husband told me what he did. Your resemblance to her really is remarkable." Lucy attempted to bring the tissue to her face but could not. Ayla sensed her distress and picked up the crumbled tissue. Lucy smiled at her feebly.

"It's the strangest thing to have your wits about you and yet be struggling to even make your body do what it needs to. I'm getting a little better each time I try though. Problem is that it's painful to move too much right now, and my hands just don't want to grip as well as they should. But the doctor said it shouldn't be too long before they get me into some sort of physical therapy program, and then I'll be able to get back to doing things normally."

Ayla nodded, admiring her tenacity. *No wonder she survived.* "I'm sure you will soon be out of here and back home," Ayla said as she attempted to comfort her.

"Oh, darling, I do hope so. There's nothing like being around *your* things in *your* place. Everybody has been real nice to me, but I would like to be able to sit on my own sofa and try to piece together the things

I can't recall. It's kinda like having something on the tip of your tongue and not being able to recall what it was. Rather nerve-racking."

"I can't even imagine," Ayla said sympathetically.

"Well, I know eventually I'm going to figure out what happened or at least I hope so. But for the meantime, tell me about yourself. All this talking has me so exhausted, and I would like to just listen to you for a while, if you don't mind."

Although Ayla wasn't really sure if Mrs. Taylor wanted the short or long version, she obliged her. She started with the city they used to live in, her friends, school, her family, and when they had moved to this town. She told of the odd looks she had received when she first moved here. About befriending Mrs. Tilly and how Sheriff Taylor had looked at her when she and her father first came to the hospital. How he had told her about the girl and how she realized a strange dream she had recently must be related. Lucy sat in silence listening to each and every word Ayla said.

"My, oh my," she said, finally letting out a deep breath. "Sounds like you have been on an adventure."

"Sometimes it feels like it," Ayla retorted. She noticed Lucy attempting to pull her thin bed sheet up and quickly lifted it up for her, stretching it over her thin frame and up past her shoulders, tucking it in to hold it in place.

"There," said Ayla, "it is rather chilly in here, if I do say so myself."

"Yes . . . it is," Lucy said, her teeth chattering a little.

"Tomorrow I'll bring you a nice blanket to put over you. That oughta keep you warm in here since they always keep hospitals so cold."

"I'd really appreciate that, Ayla."

"No problem," Ayla said, still trying to keep the conversation upbeat and positive.

"Did my husband tell you why the townsfolk look at you so oddly?" Lucy asked, her voice becoming serious.

"'Course, I look just like that girl, I suppose. What else reason would they have?"

"Guilt," Lucy said, letting the word sink in.

"Guilt?" Ayla looked at her as if she didn't fully understand.

"Yes, guilt. 'Cause they did nothing to stop it."

"Stop what, the murder?"

"Yes, in a way, or at the very least, avoid it."

"I don't understand, Mrs. Taylor. How could they have stopped anything? It wasn't any of them that killed her."

"True," Lucy replied, "but they did nothing except turn a blind eye when child services placed her back in the home when they all . . . we all knew she was being abused. Guess we figured child services knew what they were doing. Better to not get involved 'cause we thought it wasn't our problem." Lucy's lower lip quivered as she spoke. "My husband and I and a few others had made comments to their office about how we felt but did very little if anything to follow up with it and, needless to say, we all now know what happened."

"I see," said Ayla, looking at her sadly.

Mrs. Taylor continued, "Even now, because John was the one who found her, he still can't let go of his guilt and regret. He's had nightmares since that night and refuses to see a doctor about it. I assume he's still haunted by all of that because it's so painful for him."

Ayla did not know what to say. She truly felt sorry for them but especially for the little girl. No one had been there when she'd really needed them. *Was that why she was trying to speak to me?* Ayla thought. She was confused.

"I hope I haven't upset you, dear," Lucy said, jolting Ayla out of her little daydream.

"No," Ayla said, quietly still thinking about her dream. The chair was beginning to feel uncomfortable, so she stood up stretching her thin arms as far as she could and then bringing them down to her sides. "You know, Mrs. Taylor," Ayla piped up, "perhaps there is something that still can be done to help your town."

Lucy looked squarely at Ayla, though Ayla knew she did not have any idea what she was talking about, so she proceeded. "See, I overheard my dad and Sheriff Taylor discussing what was going to happen to that little boy. I think his name is Levi, and my dad was telling the sheriff when the court date was. Maybe your husband is trying to get involved in making sure he lives where he can be happy." Lucy struggled to hold back tears. Many times she and John had spoken of adoption but really didn't follow up with anything. As the years had gone by, they had laughed and cried at the idea of it, but now felt a little too old and just a bit set in their ways.

"Does your father think we have a chance?" she asked timidly.

"I haven't a clue," Ayla retorted.

"Guess I knew that was going to be your reply, but I wasn't sure if there had been a hearing or something already."

Ayla smiled back earnestly, "My dad says they usually move pretty quickly on cases involving children."

Lucy looked exhausted now and her eyelids began to droop. Walking over to her bed again, Ayla propped the pillows up and adjusted Lucy's blanket once again. "No worries now, get some sleep. We can talk tomorrow." The rest of her watch over Mrs. Taylor proved to be extremely quiet and uneventful. Though her mind raced with questions to ask her father when she returned home, she managed to quietly finish her homework and read one of the books assigned by her English teacher. As Ayla looked at the clock, a knock on the door revealed her father and Sheriff Taylor.

"Hope you're not too bored just sitting here," the sheriff said as Ayla began putting her things back in her backpack.

"Not hardly," Ayla said quietly so as not to wake Lucy. "Your wife is so strong and so sweet. In fact, I've honestly enjoyed coming to watch her."

"Really?" Sheriff Taylor said in disbelief, thinking that Ayla must have just sat in silence the majority of the time.

"Yep, we talked about lots of things, even about that little boy, Levi."

Ayla's father and Sheriff Taylor looked at one another. "What do you mean, Ayla?" her father said.

"I mean we talked about Levi, Dad. You know the little boy in the news . . . the one you and the sheriff are talking about these days. I told her that I thought Sheriff Taylor might be asking you about him so much because he wants him to go to a good home. Was I wrong? Did I say something I shouldn't?" Ayla's countenance fell, thinking that perhaps she had divulged some big secret that she shouldn't have. Her stomach felt queasy, and she sat on the chair still holding on to her backpack.

Ayla's father put his hand on her shoulder. "It's not that bad, Ayla. It's just that I'm not sure if the sheriff wanted to tell her in his own way or if he had already discussed it with her."

Sheriff Taylor smiled. "I've discussed it with her briefly when Bobby Lee was still on the loose," his head dropping and his voice becoming a whisper, "before all this, of course."

Ayla blinked her eyes, feeling a bit of relief as she heard those words. She did not want to say something that she shouldn't and, most importantly, she did not want to disappoint anyone.

"Well, there will be more time to discuss that, but I guess we can head on out and give the sheriff and his wife some privacy," Ayla's father said, letting out a small sigh as if he was getting tired.

"Okay, Dad," Ayla said.

Sheriff Taylor said good-bye as they both headed out the door.

As usual, the ride proved to be nonstop chatter as Ayla quizzed her father about little Levi.

"Why do you want to know so badly, Ayla?" her father asked after a few minutes of answering her questions.

"Well," Ayla said sheepishly, "I guess I care, that's all. The more I'm around Mrs. Taylor, I keep hoping that they can adopt that little boy and maybe their lives can be good."

"What makes you think their lives aren't good?" he retorted. "Well, except for the recent events, of course."

"I didn't mean it like that, Dad. I just think it would make it so much better."

"Oh, I see," he said and smiled. He knew Ayla. She was always intuitive when it came to other people's feelings. He figured maybe Mrs. Taylor and Ayla had spoken more than what she had mentioned to the sheriff. The conversation might prove to be more on the therapeutic level than anything. So he decided to appease her as they drove home, answering her questions and discussing procedurally how things must run their course in the judicial system. Ayla seemed fascinated, taking in every word. Soaking up the knowledge, her father could see her "wheels turning," but she did not elaborate on her thoughts or, rather, her conclusions.

Once home, she grabbed her backpack and opened the door. In an instant, she knew her mother wasn't at school. The sweet smell of garlic bread and fresh pasta filled the kitchen, and Ayla's stomach began to make noises. She instantly threw her backpack down by the laundry room and danced her way into the kitchen, stopping only to smile at her while she stood by the stove stirring a large steaming stainless steel pot that was filled with delicious noodles. Her mother smiled back tiredly and put her arms around Ayla. "Your turn, dear," she said as she hugged her tightly. "I've already hugged everybody else when they got off the school bus."

Ayla very seldom saw her since they had moved there. With her mother working and returning to college to take extra courses, Ayla had transitioned into doing most of the housework and cooking. It had proved to be difficult at first, but Ayla had soon managed to accomplish that and her homework each night. However, in the rare moments her mother had been off from school, the return was most welcome.

"I'm so glad you're home, Mom," Ayla said smiling. Her father was right behind her also nodding his gratitude.

"Well, it won't be long until I can spend a little more time with all of you. School is almost over, and then I can devote more time to you guys. Thank goodness, I have such a good husband and wonderful children. Lord knows I couldn't do it without you. Our commitment to each other makes all this possible." She turned back toward the stove and began stirring the ingredients again.

Hearing her siblings downstairs, Ayla headed down the stairs and pushed open the door of her room, halfway expecting to see them playing on her bed, but her ears had deceived her. Her room was untouched and everything was in its place, just how she had left it. *Must be playing in the other room*, Ayla thought as she fell backward onto her bed, looking at the ceiling as she landed softly on her back. The conversation with her dad and Mrs. Taylor had revealed a lot, and Ayla sighed as she replayed everything in her mind. "Now, if only I could make sense of what the dream meant," she said to herself as she pulled herself back up to sit on the edge of her bed, directly in front of the mirror. Her reflection stared back at her as if questioning her. Ayla looked at herself for a few minutes and then picked up her hairbrush to brush through her tangled hair.

The night went pleasantly as they all sat down to dinner. Ayla helped her mother with the dishes and then after taking her bath, headed to bed. Once underneath her sheets and fluffy comforter, she drifted to sleep, waking up the next day with no recollection of what, if anything, she had dreamt about.

School went by quickly and before she knew it, the last bell for the day rang loudly over the old speaker system. Like clockwork, all the students accumulated in sections nearest the double doors as the large school buses waited in line to take them all home. Ayla's father had mentioned that she would not have to watch Mrs. Taylor this evening, and Ayla couldn't help hiding her joy at being able to visit with Mrs. Tilly again. It had been awhile, and she was looking forward to telling her everything that had transpired since that time.

Though small and petite, Ayla tried to stand up on the tips of her toes in order to see over the ever-growing crowd of school kids. The school accommodated kindergarten through ninth grade, so needless to say, it was always hard locating her siblings, but Ayla was prepared to try. Perhaps it was a motherly instinct, but it made her feel good to do a quick headcount before they all got on the bus each day. Depending on whether or not she would visit Mrs. Tilly, Ayla's seat on the bus would change, and she wanted to make sure they knew where she was and whether or not she would be going home with them or staying to visit. Ayla scanned the crowd, but after a few sighs, put her tired feet back down. *Maybe they've already gotten on the bus*, she thought, and decided to quit worrying about it.

Gradually the crowd became smaller as Ayla patiently waited with other children in her grade. Some she had spoken with at the beginning of the year, others were still strangers, though the school year was almost over. Not everyone had been friendly, and though Ayla had continued to extend her infectious smile, most only stared. Ayla's recent discoveries had given her new insight about this phenomena, and it encouraged her to look up the girl that Sheriff Taylor and his wife thought she looked like. If even the sheriff could look perplexed the first time he saw her, perhaps there was some truth to her uncanny resemblance and the reason not all people had instantly warmed up to her. Though the stares were becoming far less frequent, there were still those uncomfortable moments where she still felt as if people were staring behind her back. She had reasoned that Mrs. Tilly might have some insight on the whole thing and wanted to find her siblings to let them know that she would be getting off the bus at Mrs. Tilly's house. If anybody had more details, it would be Mrs. Tilly. *She always seems to know a little of about everything,* she mused.

Suddenly, Ayla spotted the polka-dotted backpack of her younger sister, Ariel. "A-R-I-E-L!" she called out loudly. Her little sister looked back through the crowd of children and spotted her instantly, smiling as she pushed through to stand beside her. "Where's Jasper?" Ayla asked as Ariel came closer.

"I dunno know," she said looking up. A wisp of her light brown hair fell around her face as she tried to readjust the falling backpack over her shoulders once again. "I normally see him first, but I didn't notice him once I was here. Maybe he's already on the bus."

"I thought the same thing," Ayla said as she grabbed her sister's hand and moved toward the buses, still scouting the crowd for Jasper. "Maybe we should head that way."

Ariel was only a few years younger than Ayla, so for the most part, they shared clothes, toys, etc. Their youngest brother, Jasper, was just starting kindergarten and was already a handful. Both had to do a lot more chores since Jasper had been born and honestly were none too happy to have the extra responsibilities. However, as Jasper had gotten older, things around the house were much easier and enjoyable.

The walk was a long one. The bus they took to ride home was always the last in a long line of buses that pulled up in a uniform fashion by the entrance into the middle school. So as Ayla and Ariel continued to walk toward the bus, they both looked in either direction for any sign of Jasper. "Hey, how come you didn't just head to the bus?" Ariel asked puzzled.

"Well, I was thinking of—"

"Thinking of going to see that old lady again, aren't ya?" Ariel finished her sentence.

"Yep," Ayla said, looking intently into Arial's round, freckled face. "You guessed it."

Ariel smiled again, beaming that she had been right.

"Oh, look, I see Jasper . . . he's getting on the bus right now," Ayla said as she and Ariel picked up their pace to join him. Once there, they stepped up into the bus and spotted Jasper sitting with another young boy three rows down. Both seemed preoccupied in a conversation, but Ayla stopped in the aisle before arriving at her normal seat, causing Jasper to look up and find her standing there.

"Ayla," he said happily, throwing his hands around her legs in a big hug.

Ayla smiled back happily. "Good to see you too, Jasper," she responded in almost a giggle. "Wanted to tell you that I'm going to be visiting Mrs. Tilly today for a couple of hours, so Ariel and you just need to ride the bus back with everyone else to the house, okay?"

Jasper looked disappointed and shrugged his shoulders. "That means it's gonna be awhile before I have anyone to make me something to eat."

"What do you mean? Ariel can you make you some cereal or something to tide you over until I get home. I promise, I won't be that long." Ayla put her hand on his head as she spoke. Jasper nodded and resumed his conversation with his friend, though he appeared somewhat sullen. Ayla let out a small sigh and walked down the aisle until she found her row and sat down. She took her backpack off and positioning it between her feet on the floor.

Glancing around, she saw her other brothers and Ariel, who had already found her seat and was talking to one of her classmates. The bus driver finally finished loading the children and began driving away from the school. Mrs. Tilly wasn't too far of a walk from their house, which was usually one of the last houses, so Ayla hunkered down in her seat for a while and quietly daydreamed amid the constant chatter on the bus. Lost in thought, she almost didn't hear the bus driver calling her; she had told him earlier where she was to be dropped off. Someone poked Ayla on the shoulder. "Hey, the bus driver is calling for you." Ayla looked up and nodded to the young boy who spoke. She noticed they had stopped directly in front of Mrs. Tilly's house, so she quickly grabbed her backpack and waved a farewell to her siblings. Down the steps and out the door of the bus, she sprinted toward the porch where Mrs. Tilly was already sitting.

"Heavens, child. I was wondering when you were gonna visit with me again," she spoke as she fanned herself with what appeared to be nothing more than a piece of paper.

"Well," Ayla said, looking at her intently, "I would have come sooner and all except I've been tending to Mrs. Taylor, the sheriff's wife. You do know about what happened, don't you?"

"Of course, child. I make it my point to know. Why, we Southern ladies gotta stay abreast of any situation. By the way, how is she faring as of late? The news was brief about her injuries, but Myrtle Faye told me what she knew and, Lord have mercy, that poor woman could have been killed." Her face grimaced as she spoke and her beady little eyes bore into Ayla's.

Ayla wanted to laugh aloud but, out of respect, she did not. Whoever Myrtle Faye was and how in the world she could know about all of that was nothing more than amusing to her. Chances are, she had heard bits and pieces of what really happened and had woven enough of it together to actually make a story out of it and a whopper of one, no doubt. Mrs. Tilly studied Ayla's face, trying to glean her thoughts, but Ayla knew better than to be disrespectful or flippantly put off Mrs. Tilly's feelings. She had learned in the past to avoid raising anything like that up in their discussions. Mrs. Tilly was extremely sensitive, so Ayla simply nodded and sat her backpack down so that she could sit in the rocking chair next to her.

Once seated, Ayla replied, "Actually, she is doing really good. At first, I was nervous about taking care of her, but she is conscious and has even had conversations with me. Lengthy ones, mind you. The doctor is very nice, and he thinks she will be walking out of the hospital before too long." Ayla drew closer to Mrs. Tilly as she continued, "I can tell it's still difficult for her because she doesn't remember certain things that happened, and that's gotta be frustrating, you know?"

It was Mrs. Tilly's turn to nod to that one, and she grunted under her breath. "Some people forget because of their age, but I am seventy-two years old and still recall events with precise detail. Don't let anyone tell you otherwise, Ayla. Some memories are so bad that we can avoid annoying questions from people we could care less to talk to." Her fingers clutched the fan harder as she repetitiously shook it.

Guess Mrs. Tilly never heard of Alzheimer's. The small table by the rocking chairs lay barren and Ayla decided to change topics with Mrs. Tilly in the hopes that she could find out more about the murdered girl.

"Speaking of memories, Mrs. Tilly," Ayla said coyly, "there is an event around here that you haven't completely told me about yet."

Mrs. Tilly's ears perked up like a cat, she pushed herself toward the front of the rocking chair, and straightened her back. "Well, we talk about so many things, I'm not sure which one you are talking about."

Ayla was convinced that the tone of Mrs. Tilly's voice betrayed her, but she continued. "Oh, you know, the one . . ." Ayla paused. "The one about that girl around my age that was killed. Remember? You were trying to tell me something about her the other day?"

Mrs. Tilly's lower lip quivered, and she slowly adjusted herself in the rocking chair as if suddenly feeling very uncomfortable. "I've been meaning to, Ayla. It's just not easy since we really still all feel somewhat responsible for it. Truth be known, we try not to even utter her name, but I see somebody must have said something to you for you to want to know about it now."

"It was the sheriff," Ayla said, "though I don't think he wanted to talk about it either. But when he saw me with my father the first afternoon I was to watch Mrs. Taylor, he looked as if he had seen a ghost, and my father had demanded an explanation. He told my father that I look just like her so I wanted to come and ask you about it, since you seem to know everything around here and thought I looked like her too."

Mrs. Tilly did not speak. It was as if she were in deep thought over Ayla's words. A moment or two passed between them and Mrs. Tilly still refrained. Finally, Ayla broke the silence. "Well, do I look like her or not?" Mrs. Tilly rocked back and forth a few more times and then stood up, heading toward the screen door. Ayla jumped out of her chair as well, afraid that she had somehow upset the old woman. "Mrs. Tilly, Mrs. Tilly, I'm sorry if I've upset you or something," she said as she walked toward her. Mrs. Tilly did not reply as she opened the screen door and stepped inside of her home. Ayla stepped back as the screen door shut in front of her.

"So much for trying to figure any of this out," she said, berating herself under her breath. She eyed her backpack and wondered if she should just gather her things and leave. The idea had promise. She picked up her backpack, thinking that she might just leave a small note telling Mrs. Tilly that she had left and that she was sorry for anything she might have said or done to offend her.

Just then, Mrs. Tilly reappeared and opened the screen door. In her hands she had a small, dusty picture frame. "I hope you aren't leaving just yet. There is something I'd like to show you that might just answer your question."

Ayla felt a cold chill run down her back. The last time she had visited Mrs. Tilly, she had helped her put the dishes and cups away in the house and had somehow noticed a small, dusty picture frame on her way out that was turned backward. She recalled the feeling she had that day and, try as she might, she could not shake the idea that this particular picture frame was the one she had eyed. Mrs. Tilly brushed at the frame's sides, trying to clean it up before presenting it to her, though it didn't appear to do much good.

"It's okay, Mrs. Tilly," Ayla said gently. "I'm sure it will be fine." As Ayla spoke, she extended her hand toward her. Mrs. Tilly seemed disappointed, but handed Ayla the picture frame. At first, Ayla could see why Mrs. Tilly was trying so hard to brush some of the dust off. It was filthy.

A fine film had developed over the entire picture and its frame, making the dust almost appear sticky, but Ayla wasn't too bothered by this inconvenience. She was determined to get to the bottom of the story of the girl, her dream, and the importance of it all. She continued to brush at it as Mrs. Tilly had done, but a little harder and faster. The progress was slow, but eventually the dust and film began to wear away, leaving Ayla's hands filthy but the picture finally visible.

Ayla looked intently at the picture and gasped. It was just as she imagined. The image was like looking into a mirror, though the girl was slightly taller in stature and appeared to be somewhat malnourished. But yes, their resemblance was uncanny. Furthermore, there was no mistaking that the girl in her dreams was in fact the girl staring back at her from the old picture frame. Ayla's eyes welled up with tears, even though she had never met this girl. The pain and horror that she must have felt pulled at Ayla's heart, and she truly felt grieved at such a tragic loss. They were no doubt close enough in age to have been friends. Ayla looked up to see Mrs. Tilly also staring at the picture, her eyes full of sadness.

Ayla stretched her right hand out and grabbed Mrs. Tilly's feeble hand. Mrs. Tilly put her head down as if she felt ashamed. "There's more, Ayla," she began. "I guess afterward, most people felt so bad about it. You know, questioning themselves, and whether or not they could've done something and then a mix of embarrassment as the media came down here to accuse and intrude on everyone's privacy. It was downright awful. We went from sad to angry and then collectively agreed to not really talk about the whole thing ever again, telling ourselves these kinda children weren't our concern. It was just too painful." She squeezed Ayla's hand and walked back to her rocking chair.

Ayla walked beside her and sat down as well, the picture still in her hands. She studied it again and looked back at Mrs. Tilly. "So, how come you have a picture of her?"

Mrs. Tilly paused for a moment and closed her eyes as if summoning courage to speak the words. "I am . . . I mean, I was her great aunt. She and I were close or at least I thought we were. She was a lot like you, and she would come over every once in a while to visit, though she never stayed very long. After her death, I just sorta tried to put that behind me because I was too saddened to think about it. For days, I would have dreams about her until one day I decided to turn the picture around and after that, the dreams ceased. I haven't touched or dusted it since that time. That is until now," she finished.

Though Mrs. Tilly didn't realize it, she had given Ayla more information than she thought she would find. The full picture became so evident to her that she now understood what she needed to do. Gathering her thoughts, she handed the picture frame back to Mrs. Tilly and stood up, putting her hands on her hips and clearing her throat. "Mrs. Tilly, there's something I need to tell you. Now maybe you won't believe me and maybe you will. I reckon that's up to you. But I had a dream about this girl. A dream so real I was shaking when I woke up. She was trying to tell me something that at the time I didn't understand. Now, when I had this dream, I seriously thought I was losing my mind. I did not know the story of her or that she died. I didn't know that the stares I was getting from complete strangers was because I looked so much like her. But what I do know is that she came to me with a message for whatever reason that may be." Ayla paused, catching her breath. "I believe, or let's just say, I have this feeling that her appearance has something to do with that guy who killed his wife or girlfriend and left behind that little boy." Mrs. Tilly leaned closer as Ayla went on. "The sheriff and his wife are planning on going to that hearing soon to see if they can adopt him, but they are going against child services because they want to send him to family members who either can't afford to provide for him or others who live far away and never even met him."

"Good luck with that," Mrs. Tilly replied with disgust. "Child services is the one who kept putting Meg repeatedly back where she kept being abused. They act like they care, but they don't. We all should have stood up and fought them back then, and maybe her life would have been spared." Mrs. Tilly's eyes began to well up again.

"That may be true, Mrs. Tilly, but you cannot change what has happened at this point, nor should you keep beating yourself up about it. I think she wants us to stand up now . . . for the little boy. Besides, the hearing is so close and there's not much time to round people up and spread the word."

"Leave that to me," Mrs. Tilly said as she rocked back and forth, putting her fingers to her lips as if she was already making plans. "Time for you to skedaddle and get on home."

"Okay," Ayla said, grabbing her backpack and stepping off the porch, waving good-bye. It occurred to her that she hadn't given Mrs. Tilly the day of the hearing. Ayla yelled back the date and time while she continued walking. Though she wasn't sure if Mrs. Tilly heard her, she hoped so for the sheriff's sake.

Chapter 16

The Hearing

The morning of the hearing finally arrived. The weather was cold and uncommonly quiet as Ayla dressed. Her father had promised that she would be allowed to attend and would not have to go to school with her siblings. Though it had taken a bit of coaxing on her part, her father had finally thrown his hands up and relinquished. She had not slept well the night before. Normally, she would have been exhausted from the lack of sleep, but her mind continued to race. By the time she lay down, she could not manage to drift off to sleep as usual.

A quick view into her closet and Ayla decided that a small white cardigan and khaki pants would be sufficient. It was not the kind of event that required Sunday best. A nice necklace and belt would complement the classic look and add just enough without drawing attention. By the time she had finished dressing and brushing her long hair, it was almost time to leave. She felt nervous but wasn't sure why. This was not her fight and yet she felt very much a part. She could hear her father calling for her as she hurried to finish tidying up her room.

"I'm coming, Dad, just one more minute," Ayla called out from her room as she studied herself in the mirror. Closing her eyes, she said a quick prayer and ran up the stairs to meet him. Ayla's father smiled as he gathered his briefcase and car keys. Ayla bolted to the front door and within minutes they were driving to the courthouse.

After some time, Ayla could not help but blurt out the questions that were swimming in her head. "Dad, are you nervous? I mean, do you ever get nervous before going to court?"

Ayla's father continued to keep his eyes fixed on the road while speaking. "I guess I would be wrong in telling you that I don't get nervous sometimes," he replied. "But the truth is, it's not so much that I am nervous about myself . . . more that I worry others will not comprehend what I'm trying to express and therefore decide a case unwisely."

Ayla paused as she mulled over his words. "I think I understand," she said and looked back out of her window.

Her father smiled, but continued to stare at the road. The courthouse was about thirty minutes from where they lived, and as the miles passed by and the buildings of the town came into view, Ayla's heart began to beat faster again with anticipation.

Once inside the courthouse, everything suddenly became very real to Ayla. A security guard motioned them through as people put loose change, keys, phones, purses, and briefcases down a long conveyor belt, checking for anything that was not allowed in the courtroom. Ayla followed her father in line as they continued to be ushered to the appropriate courtroom. Down one of the long halls, Ayla walked alongside her father until they came to a door with the sign Courtroom D in brass lettering.

A bailiff stood near the head of the courtroom while a few attorneys walked up and down the aisles speaking to certain people who were sitting down. Ayla could not tell if they were there for this hearing or for others to be heard; she did not recognize any of their faces. But she did not wish to stare too long at them, for fear that they would be offended. Ayla felt so big and important walking behind her father and holding his briefcase and notes. She did not want to do or say anything that her father would not approve of.

Ayla's father stopped at the second row and motioned for Ayla to follow him as he took a few steps and sat down. He nodded his head at some of the attorneys she had seen earlier wave at him. "I'll take my briefcase now," he said quietly. "I need to review my notes before court begins."

Ayla slid the briefcase to him, and he quickly opened it, drawing a few documents out of it as well as his legal pad before shutting it and handing it back to her. He looked intently for a few minutes at the withdrawn documents, making a few quick notes on his legal pad before looking up just in time.

"All rise for the Honorable William M. Walter," the bailiff bellowed approaching the bench.

Judge Walter sat down, grabbed his gavel, and tapped it down loudly. "Be seated, be seated," he said sternly, looking back at the bailiff.

"Court is now in session, Judge Walter presiding," the bailiff stated as he walked to the corner of the room and positioned himself near the witness stand.

"Docket 108709, the state on behalf of the minor, Levi Putnam," Judge Walter stated as he put a stack of papers directly in front of him and began reading it aloud.

Ayla's father stood up, scanning the room for Sheriff Taylor. His fingers tapped nervously on the wooden bench. Ayla turned her head around as well, peering into the growing crowd of people but did not see him either. "Counsel, make appearances for the record," Judge Walter said, looking as if he would rather be anywhere but in court. Ayla's father moved past her as he headed to stand before the judge. Another man much older than her father also stepped up from the other side of the aisle and approached. "Terrance Whitaker, Your Honor, counsel for the state, on behalf of the minor child, Levi Putnam."

"James Abernathy, Your Honor, counsel for Sheriff John Taylor and his wife, Lucy Taylor."

Both Ayla's father and the older attorney looked at one another in distaste. Ayla's father did not care too much for Mr. Whitaker. The cases in which they had argued in the past were not pleasant, to say the least, and Ayla's father knew this one would be no different. Mr. Whitaker was a local and well-connected attorney throughout the state. However, what he lacked in true intelligence, he clearly made up in an oversized ego. He had more of a mindset to dress like a good attorney rather than actually be one. Word was that he had family members who had practiced for a long time and basically welcomed him the minute he had finally passed the bar. Once there, he had been handed numerous cases with very little effort on his part. And because of the firm's reputation, he had more or less won many cases due to intimidation or the lack of experience from less-seasoned counsel.

When Ayla's father had tried a few cases and had won them by a landslide, he made an everlasting enemy of Mr. Whitaker. "Your Honor, before we go any further, we ask that the witnesses in this matter be sequestered," Mr. Whitaker said sternly.

Ayla's father retorted, "We have no objection, Your Honor." As he spoke, his face lifted when he noticed that John and Lucy, through still in a wheelchair, had made it to the hearing.

They were his only direct examinations and the only ones he hoped would be necessary. All the others would be called by the state, and his notes for cross-examination were already seared inside his mind. He gathered the rest of his exhibits and spoke, "Your Honor, we call our first witnesses, if you are ready."

"I'm ready," Judge Walter said, appearing bored. "You do know I will need you to have them go ahead and come up to the front so that I can swear them in."

"Yes, Your Honor, we call Sheriff Taylor and his wife, Lucy Taylor." Judge Walter looked up and silently acknowledged the sheriff walking into the courtroom. Ayla watched as Sheriff Taylor slowly pushed his wife toward the witness stand and smiled as she and Lucy's eyes connected. She still seemed rather frail, but Ayla knew better. She was a fighter through and through and had, no doubt, been determined to be present today for the hearing no matter what.

Ayla's father stood beside them and stated their names aloud. The clerk slowly got up from her seat and motioned them to stand with their right hands raised as she swore them in. Judge Walter issued his order of sequestration and explained to them its purpose and meaning. The room was silent, but the sheriff nodded as he spoke as if he was already familiar with the procedure.

Ayla continued to watch them going through the formalities of calling the state's witnesses and swearing them in along the same order. Once all the witnesses had been sworn in and ushered by the bailiff to stand outside the courtroom in the hallway, Judge Walter turned to James and spoke matter-of-factly, "You may call your first witness, Counselor."

Chapter 17

On the Stand

After everyone was ushered back into the courtroom, Ayla's father called Sheriff Taylor to the stand. Ayla could see by his demeanor that he was nervous, but after a few questions from her father regarding simple things such as his full name, age, and background, he began to relax a bit and didn't seem as anxious. Next, her father began to ask questions about Lucy. Whether or not they had children and how he had first come to know the boy, Levi.

Most of the questions were answered very matter-of-factly until the line of questioning began about Levi. Ayla could see the sheriff pausing for a moment before replying about his first encounter while he and his men had investigated the death of his mother. She could see it was painful for him, as if he took her death personally. His voice resonated with sadness.

Not a single word was uttered as the crowd listened to his every word. It was as if one could feel the raw emotion with which he retold the instances where he had caught glimpses of Levi. He explained how he tried to persuade the boy's mother to leave her abusive husband, the detailed account of finding her body, and then having to contact child services in order to find some form of placement for him.

James did not deter Sheriff Taylor from speaking. He wanted Judge Walter to see just how much this little boy had become a part of his life, how passionate he had been in securing proper food, lodging, and clothes for him. He wanted to establish that there already existed a bond between them. Even Ayla could feel the tears welling up in the corner of her eyes as she listened. One would have been blind to not see his heartfelt connection to him.

Next, James questioned him about his conversations with Levi's family. "Objection, Your Honor, hearsay," Mr. Whitaker said smugly, standing partially up for a moment and quickly sitting back down as he waited on the judge's response.

James quickly turned to the judge, "Your Honor, my client, in his capacity as sheriff, had to discuss the situation of the minor child, Levi, with the next of kin after the gruesome murder of his mother. He then followed up with a report, which I will now submit as Exhibit A. In the report, he specifically addresses the other family members and the decedent's sister regarding the placement of the minor child and the involvement of child services. Though it appears hearsay, I strongly urge the court to allow my client to testify in his capacity as sheriff and further elaborate on this report, which I have now introduced, as it clearly is relevant to determining what is in the child's best interest over all."

Judge Walter shifted in his seat, appearing to weigh both arguments in his head before replying. "Objection overruled. Counsel, you may continue, though I must warn you my time is valuable to me, and I expect you to arrive at your point quickly."

"Yes, Your Honor," James Abernathy said humbly. He turned toward the sheriff again and inquired about his conversations as well as presented him with a copy of the report, which the sheriff read aloud as further evidence of his communication with Levi's family.

Mr. Whitaker sat back in his chair, immediately appearing disinterested in the sheriff's testimony, though he studied his copy of the report. James continued to question the sheriff regarding his interaction with Levi. Questions like finances, home life, family members, whether or not he had applied for placement of the child with child services, and whether or not he had complied with their background checks and home inspection were all raised. After Sheriff Taylor answered all the questions, James stepped away from the witness stand, seeing that he had established what he needed to, and looked up to the judge. "That's all, Your Honor." Looking at Mr. Whitaker, James said, "Your witness."

It was obvious that Mr. Terrence Whitaker was one of those attorneys who simply liked to be heard. He had no doubt tried many cases, and regardless of the outcome, he would simply chalk it up to experience and what he called "honing his skills." Being part of a firm that already gave him such a handsome salary, the outcome hardly mattered to him, as he had agreed to do a favor for the attorney who had originally been assigned to this case. And truth be known, he had figured that the murder of this little boy's mother and his situation might have some media still lingering about that might get him some "air time." As he smirked at the papers in his hand, he pushed himself up rather loudly from his seat and oozed his way toward the witness stand where Sheriff Taylor still sat. Of course, all of that was simply his way of drawing attention and, as usual, it worked.

He had perfected his dance around the courtroom even if his words were meaningless and empty as the feelings he attempted to display. "Sheriff Taylor, my name is Terrence Whitaker. I represent the state in the matter of the minor child, Levi Putnam. But I presume you already know that. So, I'm going to get started so the judge can finish up that game of golf he owes me." As he spoke, he looked at Judge Walter and smiled. Of course, this did not go unnoticed by Ayla or her father, but both held their composure. Mr. Whitaker's face beamed as he looked back at the sheriff and then quickly at the report, which had already been introduced into evidence moments before.

"So, Sheriff. How long you been in law enforcement?"

Sheriff Taylor closed his eyes for a moment and replied, "Seven years as a deputy, almost fifteen years as a sheriff."

"Why did you close your eyes when I asked the question?"

"Because I've been in law enforcement so long that I had to think about it."

Mr. Whitaker didn't miss a beat. "Fair enough, fair enough. Now out of all those years, how many of them have you had to deal with a murder or two?"

"Hmmm, I'd have to say less than seven or eight as sheriff."

"And how many of those did you personally handle, Mr. Taylor . . . I apologize . . . Sheriff?"

"Uh, well if you mean go and actually meet the coroner to where it took place and all, I'd say about half."

"Half, eh, half of seven or half of eight?" Mr. Whitaker asked sarcastically.

"Objection, Your Honor," James stated loudly, "this line of questioning is irrelevant."

The judge looked at Mr. Whitaker, waiting to hear his reply.

"Your Honor," he said dryly, "I also, just like counsel for the sheriff, do have a valid point to make, which is very relevant to this matter, and I also request a bit of patience from this honorable court."

Judge Walter looked at him and James. "Objection overruled. I'll allow it, but again with the understanding that this is not going to take all day, Counsel," his face contorting into an exaggerated yawn as he spoke.

"Sheriff Taylor, you may answer the question," Judge Walter said, turning toward him, still yawning.

"Well, I reckon it would be more like four murders."

"And out of those murders, did you ever have to seek counseling afterward?"

Sheriff Taylor hung his head down as he spoke. "Yes."

"Yes, you said?" Mr. Whitaker asked, raising his voice loudly as if exposing a secret.

"Yes," Sheriff Taylor said again, looking at him and then towards James apologetically.

"And do you recall the cases that were the reason for you seeking psychological intervention?"

"Well, now, it wasn't an interven—" Sheriff Taylor tried to say, but Mr. Whitaker stopped him abruptly.

"Just answer the question, yes or no, you remember?"

"Yes, I remember. It was a case involving a young girl. It was very tough for me, but that was a long time ago."

"Did it involve child services?"

"Yes."

"Interesting . . . and did you have a discussion with anyone who worked for child services after the murder?"

"I had discussions before and after, but no one listened."

"*Hmph.* Sounds like you have a personal problem with child services?"

"I didn't say that. I just think somebody didn't do his job, that's all."

"Oh, I am beginning to see . . . and you think that child services is not doing its job in this case either?"

"I didn't say that," Sheriff Taylor said, obviously getting a little aggravated at the direct onslaught of the attorney's accusations.

"Okay, okay, calm down, Sheriff. Let me ask you then, do you think child services has done everything it could have and are supposed to be doing for this little boy?"

"I don't know."

"Do you still think about the other case or have any problems with dealing with emotions that we should know about? Things that might not make you the best person to be raising a small boy such as Levi who also is dealing with the tragic loss of his mother?"

Sheriff Taylor felt boxed in and unsure how to answer. He knew they would question Lucy and the truth sooner or later was going to come out. He still had nightmares, still felt a sense of guilt, and yet he knew that as upsetting as the little girl's murder had been for him, he truly believed he could, and would, do whatever he needed to make little Levi's life better.

A long pause ensued and Mr. Whitaker was about to ask the question for a second time, but Sheriff Taylor spoke softly. "Yes, it's true. I do sometimes have nightmares about it. Being a sheriff doesn't excuse you from just being plain human. It was sad and in my honest opinion could have been avoided. But I'm not unable to do my job as sheriff of this town because of it, and I'm not unable to love my wife and provide for us, nor am I unable to care for a child whom I have come to love and desire to care for. That's all I want for him. That out of all of this he can be somewhere happy."

Mr. Whitaker looked up at the judge. "That's all," he said, looking upset at having been unable to keep the sheriff from talking and feeling somewhat defeated. Ayla smiled as she squeezed her father's hand.

"You may step down," Judge Walter uttered. Sheriff Taylor stepped down from the witness stand and walked toward the hallway.

"We call Mrs. Lucy Taylor to the stand, Your Honor," Mr. Abernathy called out as he approached the judge.

As Sheriff Taylor opened the large wooden doors out of the courtroom, one of the bailiffs was slowly wheeling his wife in. Their eyes met for a moment, and she smiled encouragingly at him. James wasted no time in helping the bailiff position her near the witness stand and began his questioning. A long string of basic questions ensued, much like the opening ones answered by the sheriff. At times, James would pause for a moment while Lucy struggled to answer some of them. Finally, seeing the frustration on her face, he asked, "Are you all right, Mrs. Taylor? We all are fully aware of the situation you have been through and make no mistake, want to accommodate you in any way that we can."

Lucy looked at James and smiled gratefully. "Thank you," she said, "but I'll be fine; I just have some difficulty in expressing my thoughts. My doctor said it should get better in time, so I guess I'm just a little upset that I'm having such difficulty answering the questions. If you will just give me a few moments, I think I can continue."

Judge Walter nodded sympathetically and everyone waited for a couple of minutes before James continued. "Do you believe that you are fully capable of taking care of this child, Mrs. Taylor?"

"Yes, of course," she replied.

"And do you know of anything that would prevent you and your husband from raising this child and providing him with all that he needs?"

"No, I do not," Mrs. Taylor said matter-of-factly.

"That's all, Your Honor," James said once again and nodded for Mr. Whitaker to begin his questioning.

"I only have a couple of questions to ask this witness, Your Honor," Mr. Whitaker said, not even bothering to get out of his chair. "Mrs. Taylor, does your husband have or has he had trouble dealing with any of the cases he has ever worked on, specifically any murder cases that you yourself are aware of?"

Lucy bit her lip as she appeared to fumble for a response, "Yes."

"And tell me how many children have you raised, Mrs. Taylor?" Mr. Whitaker said, eyeing her.

"Well . . . none," she said.

"That's all, Your Honor." Mr. Whitaker smiled sardonically at James.

"You may step down, Mrs. Taylor, but seeing as how you were never in the witness stand, I guess I should simply allow you to return to the hall," Judge Walter bellowed as he adjusted his cloak.

Mr. Whitaker wasted no time after she had left the courtroom. "Your Honor, the state calls Roberta Ross to the stand." A moment later, a large woman in her mid-fifties entered the courtroom with a stack of paperwork in her arm, which she placed on the table in front of Mr. Whitaker, and walked toward the witness stand. Her hair was disheveled, and the stern look on her face made her look more menacing. "Please state your full name for the court," Mr. Whitaker stated as he propped his arm against the witness stand.

"R-O-B-E-R-T-A Ross."

"And, Ms. Ross, how long have you been working for the state and child services?"

Ms. Ross looked up. "Twenty-three years," she replied tiredly.

"Twenty-three years," Mr. Whitaker echoed. He looked at her and then to the judge as if to make sure everyone had heard her response.

"Yes sir, twenty-three years," she stated again.

"And of the twenty-three years, how many times have you placed a child in the home of someone who was not related to them? If you need me to refresh your memory, I have a complete list of the names of all children who have been placed in homes beginning in 1972 to date, a copy of which I will supply to counsel for Sheriff Taylor and his wife and now introduce as Exhibit B."

Mr. Whitaker handed a copy to Judge Walter and brought the additional one to Ms. Ross, who barely glanced at it as she spoke. "None," she said and straightened her back.

"None," Mr. Whitaker said and handed the copy back to the clerk for the record. "Is that because none of these cases involved someone other than a family member trying to gain custody?"

"No," Ms. Ross responded, "I wouldn't say that."

"Then why is it, Ms. Ross, that the state felt it best to place these children with other family members when a domestic situation occurred in which they could no longer reside in the current home?"

"Well, the state is very clear about our duties and the welfare of the children. It has been determined that they are usually better in a home of another family member as opposed to a stranger. So we feel that the minor child should be placed in the home of another family member who, in this case, resides in another state but who is willing to comply with our requirements if necessary."

Mr. Whitaker paused, studied his notes, and picked up another small stack of documents, bringing it to Ms. Ross. "Now, Ms. Ross," his voice getting a little louder, "can you tell me what this is?"

Ms. Ross took the papers being handed to her as she replied, "This is Sheriff Taylor's application for child placement."

Mr. Whitaker turned toward Judge Walter and the clerk. "Your Honor, the state would also like to introduce the sheriff's application for child placement as Exhibit C." Mr. Whitaker continued to walk, handing Judge Walter and James a copy of the documents.

Walking back to the witness stand, he gave a copy to Ms. Ross as he asked her to read a couple of sections on the last couple of pages. "Ms. Ross, I want you to turn to page 5 and at the very bottom of the page, there are two sections under No. 43 and 44, respectively. I would appreciate if you would read each question and their answers one at a time and loudly so everyone that is present can hear you." Ms. Ross nodded in agreement and began to read aloud.

"Have you or anyone in your household suffered from any type of mental conditions, which would prevent you from adequately caring for the children? The answer was no" Ms. Ross continued as Mr. Whitaker motioned with his hands for her to keep reading.

"Have your or anyone in your household taken any type of parenting courses, classes, or had experiences with children, which you or they would like us to consider? The sheriff wrote as an answer that he had not but that his wife has frequently worked with children."

Mr. Whitaker stretched out his long, wiry hand and took the documents back from Ms. Ross as he spoke. "So, Ms. Ross, having considered the state's determination or, let me rephrase that, its position regarding preference of family members, the sheriff's application, and his own admission of nightmares, which he previously testified to, and he and his wife's inexperience with children, is it safe to say your opinion is that it is not in the best interest of this child to be placed in their care?"

"I would say that, yes."

"That's all, Your Honor. Your witness, Counsel."

Chapter 18

Levi Has a Home

Ayla watched as her father stood up and straightened his tie. He quickly grabbed Sheriff Taylor's application and approached the witness stand. "Ms. Ross, are you familiar with the application that Sheriff Taylor submitted to your office?"

"Yes, I believe so."

"Good, and in that application, besides what Mr. Whitaker is implying, did you see anything that would indicate instability?"

"Technically, no."

"Inadequate housing or funds?"

"Um, no."

"What about noncompliance of the state's procedures when applying for the child placement program, such as background checks and inspection of home meetings subsequent with case workers?"

"No."

"No to which ones, Ms. Ross?"

"No to everything you just said. The sheriff and his wife did comply with all of our requirements in order to be considered for placement of a child. We just prefer that the children be placed with other family members."

"You prefer?" James said loudly, turning to face the ever-growing crowd in the courtroom. "It was my impression that while *you* may prefer that, and in most instances is perfectly acceptable, what is in the child's best interest should not be defeated because of outdated procedures or what *you* prefer, Ms. Ross"

Ms. Ross was visibly upset by James' remark, and her eyes hid none of her disdain for him. "Well, Mr. Abernathy, we've been doing the same thing for many years now, and—"

James cut her off, "That's no excuse, Ms. Ross. These cases are delicate as are the children who are in need, and there is no indication that Sheriff Taylor and his wife are unable to provide everything this small boy will need. The sheriff's occasional nightmares, if you will, has done nothing to prevent him from doing his job and providing for himself and his wife, which brings me to my final question. Do you truly feel that it is in the best interest of this little boy that he be placed with family members miles away with whom he has had no interaction his entire life just because it's been your procedure to do so?"

Ms. Ross looked down at her hands and paused before she spoke. "I really don't know, I guess so."

James let a long moment of silence pass between them before he spoke, "That's all, Your Honor," and then he sat back down.

"Ms. Ross, you may step down," Judge Walter said quickly. "Counsel, you may begin with your closing arguments."

Ayla watched as her father awkwardly straightened his tie once again before standing up and walking toward the center of the courtroom. All eyes bore into him as he spoke. His voice was soft, but firm. His plea was simple. It was for the life of Levi. It wasn't about whether or not the state was wrong in their procedures, but more so that this one decision was the absolute turning point for the little boy's life. Would the decision be the best for him and who would provide him with what he needed to mature into a good man? He slowly and methodically retold the history of Levi's life prior to his poor mother's fate. How he had personally seen the little boy make a connection with Sheriff Taylor and the way that both the sheriff and his wife had also began to care deeply for him. All the witnesses had returned to the courtroom. As Ayla listened, she looked at the crowd and her eyes fell on the sheriff, his wife, and Ms. Ross. She could feel the tears welling up, and she tried her best to dry them with her sleeve.

Only Judge Walter and Mr. Whitaker seemed unmoved by such a passionate plea. As Mr. Abernathy finished, Mr. Whitaker stood up. His face was contorted into more of a grimace than anything. His voice was louder and his tone more sarcastic in nature. Even his walk to the center of the courtroom, where James had just stood, was more of a saunter than an actual walk.

"Hmph," Ayla said under her breath, and folded her arms. Mr. Whitaker's words were more like a rehearsed speech than the emotional and eloquent plea of her father. He argued the state's procedures, the total amount of children who had been placed into the homes of family members within the last decade, and the "nightmares" Sheriff Taylor had failed to list in his application. He vehemently argued that to allow this would upset the procedures that had for so long been in place. There was not a single mention of anyone's feelings in the matter, not even Levi's. It was almost as if he were just another statistic, just another name in a long list and nothing more.

As she listened, she could feel the anger burning inside of her. How anyone could be so cold and unfeeling was beyond her. She wondered if Mr. Whitaker had any children of his own, but quickly concluded that such a thing would be impossible for such a calloused man. Once finished, he walked back to his desk.

"The state rests, Your Honor," he retorted as if it had been an afterthought.

Judge Walter's expression remained unchanged. "Mr. Abernathy, is there anything more you would like to add before I render my decision on the matter? I've got plenty of other matters on my docket, so if you don't mind, I would like to move this along."

James stood up as he spoke. "No, Your Honor, we do not. We believe that this matter should be considered on the basis of what is in the best interest of the child, Levi Putnam, and not on outdated procedures that work to exclude the specific emotional and situational issue within each individual case."

Judge Walter's eyebrows furrowed at Mr. Abernathy's last comments, and he looked down as he reviewed the exhibits before him. The courtroom was quiet as everyone awaited his decision. Ayla had hoped that his face might reveal which way he had decided, but it did not. His weathered face remained elusive as he continued to look down at the documents, much to Ayla's disappointment. As everyone waited, Ayla closed her eyes and quickly prayed. She could feel the intensity in the room as the collective courtroom held its breath. Ayla continued to stare at the judge until she saw him clear his throat and begin to speak.

"Counsel, having considered the law, the argument of counsel, and the testimony of the witnesses presented in this matter, I have made my decision and will issue my ruling in this matter at this time . . . I hereby grant that the child, Levi Putnam, be placed in the custody of Sheriff John Taylor and his wife, Lucy Taylor."

The courtroom erupted with applause.

"Order . . . order . . . I haven't finished," he said gruffly. The applause died down and once again a hush fell over the courtroom. "Said placement to commence immediately with the following conditions: Sheriff Taylor and his wife will submit to any and all future requirements and/or procedures with child services. Secondly, they will routinely discuss progress and/or problems with the minor child. Lastly, they will allow reasonable visitation with family members of the minor child. Counsel for the sheriff will submit this in writing to my office within three days from today's date."

"Yes, Your Honor," James said quickly.

Judge Walter took the gavel and dropped it loudly, "Okay, gentleman, it looks like we are done here."

Again the deafening applause rang out amongst the crowd as the sheriff wheeled his wife toward Ayla and her father. Both were smiling from ear to ear. Out of the corner of her eye, Ayla could see Mr. Whitaker grabbing his documents as he and Ms. Ross quickly exited the courtroom. She closed her eyes and whispered, "Thank you."

That night, Ayla could hardly sleep. It had been such an emotional and exciting day. She could not wait to go visit with Mrs. Tilly again and talk to her about all that had transpired. Perhaps even Mrs. Taylor would let her come visit from time to time. Thoughts swirled in her head until finally she drifted to sleep and began to dream.

Suddenly, she was back in the fields where she had last seen the poor girl who not long ago had frightened her. But this time, she did not feel afraid and, once again, tried to speak to her, tell her that everything was okay now. Ayla scanned the field and saw the girl in the distance. She was determined to catch her as she ran through the fields in that direction.

Finally, she came to an abrupt stop in front of the wispy silhouette, her heart beating wildly. She was so close now and felt cold the nearer she came. But as Ayla opened her mouth to speak, only the words of the apparition resonated, "I so am glad your heart listened, but there is still more, much more." Her voice cascaded over the wind.

Ayla awoke not long after, startled and still very cold. She pulled the blanket up to her neck and tried to warm herself. A single tear fell from her face as she called out into the darkness, "I promise."

***

Two months later, Ayla, her family, Mr. and Mrs. Taylor, and Levi all stood in unison at the graves of both Meg Flander and Christine Putnam, Levi's mother, to pay their respects. After laying flowers, Sheriff Taylor spoke, "You wanna hear something crazy? Ever since we have had Levi, I've not had a single nightmare. For the life of me, I can't figure that out. But I guess it doesn't matter, just as long as I'm finally sleeping."

Ayla was the first to respond. "I don't think that's crazy at all because I think she's finally gone now. You know . . . at peace. I saw her again in my dreams right after the hearing, and she told me something that I think she wants me to do."

Ayla's father and Sheriff Taylor looked at her incredulously, both replying at the same time, "What was that?"

Ayla smiled as she spoke. "To *save them, save them all.*" And with that, she put her arms around Levi and squeezed him tightly.

THE END

CPSIA information can be obtained at www.ICGtesting.com
Printed in the USA
LVOW12*2158271014

410792LV00002B/6/P